RENEWALS: 691-4574
DATE DUE

**WITHDRAWN
UTSA LIBRARIES**

Town Building
on the
Colorado Frontier

Town Building on the Colorado Frontier

Kathleen Underwood

University of New Mexico Press : Albuquerque

Library of Congress Cataloging-in-Publication Data

Underwood, Kathleen Hill, 1944–
  Town building on the Colorado frontier.

  Bibliography: p.
  Includes index.
  1. Cities and towns—Colorado—Growth—Case studies. 2. Frontier and pioneer life—Colorado—Grand Junction—Case studies. 3. Grand Junction (Colo.)—Social conditions. I. Title.
HT371.U515   1987   307.7'62'0978817   86-30868
ISBN 0-8263-0951-8

Copyright © 1987 by the University of New Mexico Press.
All rights reserved.
First edition

To the memory of
Fern Parry Hill, Robert B. Hill,
and Robin Hill Levine

CONTENTS

Illustrations viii
Tables ix
Acknowledgments xi
Introduction xv
Prologue 1
1. Forging the Community: Town Builders and Family Men 7
2. Weaving the Economic Fabric 23
3. Community Decision Making 51
4. Population Turnover and the Social Arena 75
5. Social Interaction: Inside and Outside the Family 95
Conclusion: Grand Junction and the Genesis of the Small Town 107
Appendix 1. Social Network Analysis 117
Appendix 2. Estimates of Voter Eligibility 121
Appendix 3. Voluntary Associations 129
Notes 133
Bibliography 161
Index 175

ILLUSTRATIONS

Figures

Figure 1. Population Distribution for Grand Junction, the West, and the United States	15
Figure 2. Relative Importance of Occupational Categories, 1885 and 1900	31
Figure 3. Men's and Women's Affiliate Network, 1885	102
Figure 4. Men's Affiliate Network, 1900	104
Figure 5. Women's Affiliate Network, 1900	105
Figure 6. Matrix of Social Connections	118
Figure 7. Estimated Population Increase, 1881 to 1920	122
Figure 8. Percentage Eligible to Vote in Regular Elections	123
Figure 9. Population Eligible to Vote in Indebtedness Elections	126

Maps

Map 1. The Rocky Mountain West	xxii
Map 2. Colorado's Western Slope	10

TABLES

Table 1.	Marital Status of the Population, Age 15 and Over	16
Table 2.	Household Structure and Composition, 1885 and 1900	17
Table 3.	Age, Life Cycle, and Occupation of Property Holders	35
Table 4.	Age, Life Cycle, Occupation, Wealth, and Networks of Emigrants and the Stable Core	77
Table 5.	Length of Residence for 1885 Families	79
Table 6.	Age, Life Cycle, Occupation, Wealth, and Networks for Transient and Resident Families	80
Table 7.	Age, Life Cycle, Occupation, and Wealth of Male Participants, 1882 to 1885	85
Table 8.	Age, Life Cycle, Occupation, and Wealth of Male Participants, 1897–1900	86
Table 9.	Age, Life Cycle, Family Occupation, and Wealth of Female Participants, 1882 to 1885 and 1897 to 1900	91
Table 10.	Kin Relationships for Men and Women, 1885 and 1900	97
Table 11.	Estimated Eligible Voters at Municipal, General, and County Elections Compared to Actual Turnout	124
Table 12.	Estimated Eligible Voters in Elections Incurring Municipal Debts	127
Table 13.	Population Persistence, 1885 to 1900	151

ACKNOWLEDGMENTS

Over the past several years, it has been useful for me to view this research and writing as an apprenticeship. When I began, I had an idea of what the end product should be, but few of the skills necessary to create it. Without the guidance and patience of several scholars, those skills might never have been acquired. Norris Hundley guided me as I defined the questions for this study—a process that took more months than I care to remember. Yet the time was necessary for my intellectual development, and he never suggested that I hurry. I continue to be motivated by his rigorous regard for historical inquiry. His passion for precise writing furnishes a model for my expression, and I hope his example is reflected in this work. From drawing diagrams on his office blackboard, as I outlined my research, to criticizing each chapter, Eric Monkkonen willingly consulted with me when this book was beginning. Discussions with Kathryn Kish Sklar during my first year of graduate training (and in subsequent years) raised the issue of the impact of the family on frontier town building. Seminars with Georges Sabagh provided me with both the theoretical perspectives and the methodological tools of historical demography.

Several scholars and friends commented on earlier versions of this manuscript, and in almost every case, I heeded their advice. Alice Reich and Allan G. Bogue read the entire manuscript, and Leslie Page Moch and Robert B. Fairbanks commented on portions of it. James O. Huff will always ask the toughest questions; however, since he helped me see that such questions may be restated as problems and that problems have solutions, those questions are not so daunting. I continue to draw with great frequency on Anne Sigismund Huff's uncanny ability to focus attention on any inquiry, specifically as well as generally. Gary D. Stark, a relative newcomer to the study of frontier towns, has nevertheless shown himself to have what might be called a "pioneer spirit" in his concern for graceful composition.

Generous support from the University of Texas at Arlington's Organized Research Fund facilitated the completion of this study by providing a summer of additional research in Colorado as well as the opportunity to expose my study to the scrutiny of others at scholarly meetings. The Organized Research Fund also underwrote the artwork and photographs in this book. Trish Caldwell designed the original maps, and Eleanor Forfang drafted the first charts and graphs. Yafit Avizemal updated their work and rendered several new figures.

Many people in Grand Junction, my hometown, expedited this research. Several times I called upon Judy Prosser, archivist at the Museum of Western Colorado, to set aside what she was doing and pay attention to my questions—which she did graciously. Earl Sawyer, Mesa County Clerk, and his able staff guided me to many valuable sources. Gena Harrison, Mesa County Treasurer, supplied me with a desk in her office throughout the several weeks that it took me to copy tax records. Neva Lockhart, Grand Junction City Clerk, also generously furnished her time, access to the town's documents, and work space. Since the project began, Alice Sigismund Nikkel has played an important part in this research, and it has been of immeasurable value to have in Grand Junction a trustworthy friend who would track down a necessary piece of information on short notice.

My love of history was learned quite literally at my mother's knee. She preferred reading to almost everything else, and she instilled in all her children a quest for knowledge and the desire to ask questions. Had times been different, the first professional historian in my family would have been Fern Parry Hill. I have dedicated this book to her, to my father Robert B. Hill, and to my sister Robin Hill Levine. Though none of them will ever read the book, they gave me the will to finish whatever I started; with Robin, that will was always tempered with laughter.

As I have researched and written this study about pioneers creating a community where none had previously existed, I have come to value the members of my community—a community that sometimes lacks a spatial dimension but a community nevertheless. The people in my community know who they are, and so do I.

INTRODUCTION

"It is the small town . . . that is our heredity."[1]

Small towns represent a shared experience for most Americans—either as a reality for those who have lived in them or as an image found in the pages of American literature and drama. In 1976, a *Time* magazine article, entitled "Why Small-Town Boys Make Good," found that virtually all the presidential hopefuls had small-town origins. In that article, historian Daniel Boorstin suggested that small-town life is "more graspable," and journalist Bill Moyers observed that "people in towns get a better sense of themselves, their places. The families stay closer, the landmarks last longer."[2]

Daily life in small towns has been the focus of several writers. Best known, perhaps, is Gopher Prairie, the town that Sinclair Lewis fled; but life in Spoon River was equally hard for Edgar Lee Masters. Portrayals of the small town have not been monolithic, however, and writers like Zona Gale and Booth Tarkington have described more friendly settings.[3] As Richard Lingeman and Anthony Channel Hilfer have suggested, there is a historiography of sorts in the small-town literature, influenced by the personal experiences of writers and the larger events in their world. In the 1880s and early 1890s, writers described the bleak aspects of small-town life, but that view became more optimistic and friendly in the first decade of the twentieth century. Then, about the time of the First World War, writers again saw small towns as hopeless and unpleasant places; but this view changed again in the 1930s.[4] At present, Americans seem to prefer the friendly view of small towns, as evidenced by such recent best sellers as ". . . *And Ladies of the Club*" and *Lake Wobegon Days*.[5]

Regardless of the prevailing climate of opinion concerning small-town life, its importance is compelling as a focus of attention. Not only has the small town been a setting for writers of fiction; it has been of interest to scholars as well. Sociologists, in particular, have studied the nature of society in small centers, and other social scientists have focused on aspects of contemporary community life such as leadership and economic functions.[6] Historians, too, have been interested in the small town, but that interest has been primarily confined to small towns of the colonial and early national eras.[7] By comparison, the small town of the middle and late nineteenth century has attracted far less attention from historians, perhaps because the last quarter of the nineteenth century and the early years of the twentieth century witnessed rapid industrialization and considerable migration to metropolitan areas.[8] Robert Wiebe has argued that during this period small, traditional, and autonomous "island communities" perished. Page Smith contends that sometime about the turn of the century, the small town "vanished." Certainly, the theme of urbanization has been a major concern of scholars in the twentieth century, and George Mowry, in the introduction to *The Urban Nation*, succinctly suggests why: "Sometime between 1915 and 1920 the old rural majority living on the producing land, or close to it in small towns and villages, became a minority."[9]

The belief that small towns disappeared is erroneous. As late as 1920, about a third of the nation's population resided in communities of less than ten thousand.[10] Nearly all of those communities were, and many still remain, small centers of population. Of the 1,507 places designated as urban by the Bureau of the Census in 1890, for example, 1,150 (76.3 percent) were towns of less than ten thousand people and more than half were places of between twenty-five hundred and five thousand population. As recently as 1970, 67 percent of the "urban" centers had populations of less than ten thousand. Indeed, during this century, five times as many small towns have been incorporated as have failed.[11]

Two biases, I think, help to explain the mistaken belief that small towns have disappeared. First, small towns are statistically invisible. In 1906, the U.S. Bureau of the Census adopted a rural–urban classification system; since then, any place with less than twenty-five hundred people has been labeled as rural and every other place is considered to be urban.[12] This grouping implies no significant differences between a town of, say, five thousand and a city of one hundred thousand or more. Clearly, the Census Bureau's differentiation is not in accordance with present notions of *urban,* nor does it conform to definitions of that term utilized by most social scientists.[13] The rural–urban classification also masks an important consideration: While there was extensive population redistribution in the latter years of the nineteenth century, many people chose to remain in or to move to relatively small communities.

The second bias contributing to the scholarly neglect of small towns stems from the underlying assumption that urbanization is an orderly progression beginning with a village that grows in population and function to metropolitan status. Those settlements that achieve such status have been called successes and the rest failures.[14] This book, however, rejects the notion that urbanization follows a linear process. Instead, I contend that although small towns were a distinct part of the urbanization taking place in late nineteenth-century America, they provided for many people an attractive alternative to the massive growth occurring in large metropolitan centers. While many people contributed to the expansion of those large centers, others moved to or remained in small locations, and still others migrated to new settlements that were being built in frontier areas. The history of the American West has been closely associated with town (and in some cases, eventual urban) development, and it is the settlement of new towns in the West—especially those that remained small for relatively long periods of time—that interests me. Such settlements suggest that many Americans continued to identify opportunity with small towns at a time when others sought advancement in rapidly growing cities. Put another way, alongside the larger impulses toward urbanization and the decline of small centers in some regions, there was vigorous community building going on as settlers tried to create new towns on the frontier. My research focuses on these smaller, neglected communities by providing a case study of the settlement and development of Grand Junction, Colorado—one small town on the late nineteenth-century frontier.

The purpose of this study is to describe and analyze the frontier town-building experience, and thereby to identify the salient characteristics in the evolution of a community from a nascent pioneer settlement to that stage where the town's continued existence seemed assured. I suggest that pioneer settlements of the late nineteenth century possessed distinctive social, political, and economic characteristics that gradually changed as the residents gained confidence and came to see themselves as members of a permanent community—a small town. That confidence, in large part, emerged as their community's identity developed.

As pioneers moved into new areas, they confronted a multitude of problems, with most of them common to all frontiers (for example, law and order, how to make a living, and when to establish churches and schools). It is in the solution to such problems that community building takes place. Some problems had easy solutions to which pioneers readily agreed, while others sparked conflict; yet out of this dynamic problem solving, a community identity was forged.

To describe and analyze the nature of life in a pioneer settlement and small town of the late nineteenth century, I have focused on the primary units of social organization: economic, participatory, and familial activities. Economic activities include business diversity, occupational structure, and property distribution. Participation, as analyzed here, means the extent to which men and women engaged in political decision making and in the activities of nonpolitical voluntary associations. The family provides a third focus for my study. The family has long been recognized as a pervasive component of most nineteenth-century communities, yet only recently has its relationship to economic and associative institutions come under scrutiny. Moreover, when family and participation are examined, the role of women in frontier community building becomes evident. Demographic analysis underlies my study of social organization. Like other historians who study the frontier, I am interested in understanding the problem of population turnover.

My intent is to provide more than another microstudy of frontier town building, although a paucity of such research exists for the area west of the one-hundredth meridian. Therefore, I have deliberately structured this study in a manner that facilitates comparisons with the findings of others. Only through such comparisons can generalizations about "the frontier" or "the small town" be made. I seek neither to defend the small town nor to attack it; rather, I aim to use the methods and sources of social history to understand daily life in a developing community. Instead of allowing novelists, poets, and playwrights—especially those who deserted their hometowns—to determine what life was like there, I suggest that we examine the lives of those often inarticulate women and men who stayed to build a community.

Although the evolution of the community itself is the primary focus of this study, the lives of several settlers provide windows on that community. In terms of age, gender, and occupation, these settlers typify Grand Junction. James W. Bucklin was one such person. A young attorney, Bucklin moved first to Denver and then to Grand Junction, where he established his practice. When he settled in Grand Junction, Bucklin was single, as were many pioneers; within a decade he was married, and he had also become active in Grand Junction politics, spearheading the drive for municipal ownership of the community's water supply. The Ackerman family—J. H., Ella Belle, and their two children—also typify a segment of Grand Junction's early population. On arrival, J. H. established a thriving construction business, later shifted to groceries, and then to a clothing business. Ella Belle was active in Grand Junction's voluntary community, and involved in the family grocery store. During these initial years, the Ackermans expanded their family as four more children were born to them. Bucklin and the Ackermans, and some others like them, stayed in Grand Junction for more than two decades, and thus promoted the stability of the community. Since none of the pioneer settlers left diaries or other biographical accounts, I have had to piece together their lives through such impersonal sources as the census, marriage and death reports, tax records, and newspaper accounts.

With this study of Grand Junction I seek to broaden our understanding of urbanization in the late nineteenth century by providing a detailed account of the nature of life in a frontier small town. I begin with Grand Junction's inception, and end when the town's continuance seems assured. I identify indices that mark the transition from a pioneer settlement to a small town. Certainly, few areas west of the Appalachian Mountains can look to long periods when towns were not a significant feature of settlement. I argue that in the late nineteenth century those towns provided an alternative to the massive urbanization that has been more commonly associated with that period.

Town Building
on the
Colorado Frontier

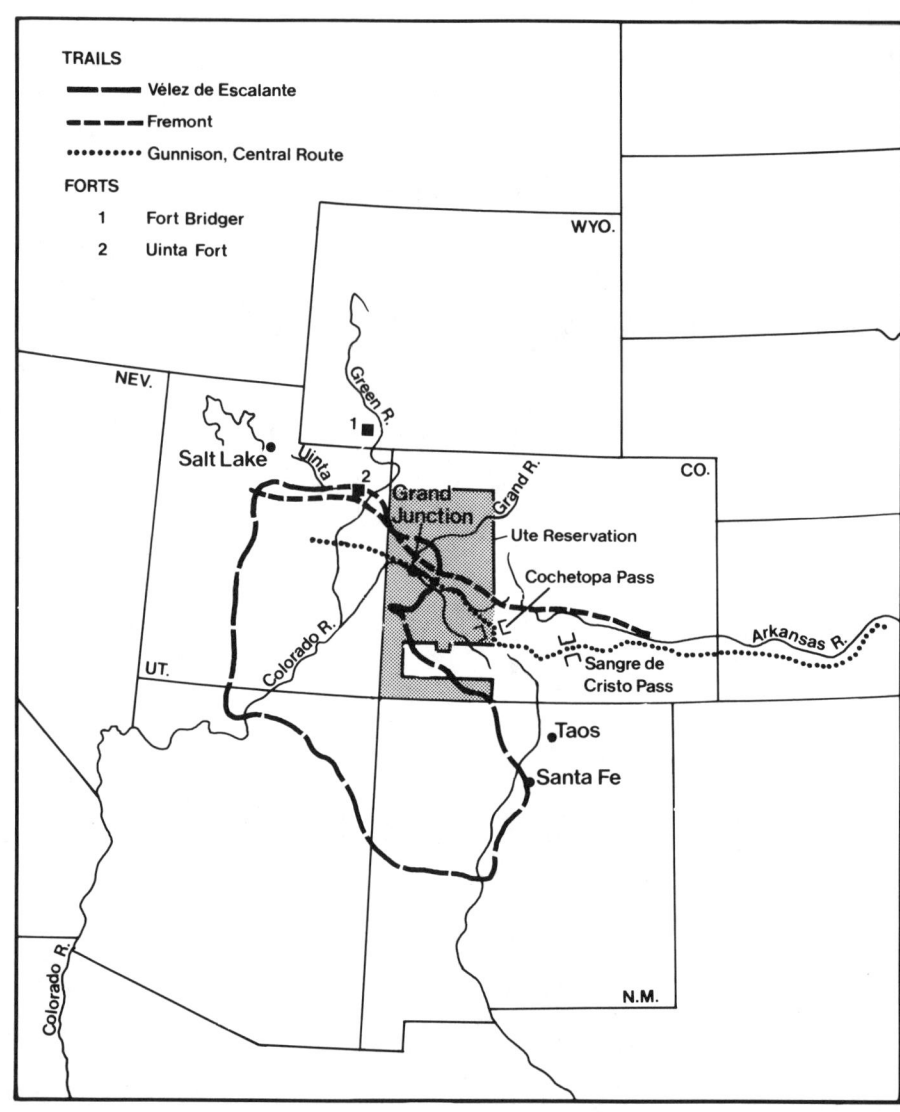

The Rocky Mountain West

PROLOGUE

"The Utes Must Go!"[1]

The nomadic Utes regarded the intermountain West as their homeland. Principally, they roamed what is now eastern Utah and western Colorado. Except for fur-trading posts, the Utes had little contact with whites until the Mexican cession in 1848. The following year, the United States government initiated a policy that separated the Utes in Utah from those in Colorado. This separation, according to anthropologist Joseph G. Jorgensen, was "somewhat artificial, for historic Ute bands did not respect [such] boundaries." More important for them than the territorial partition, however, was the encroachment by whites. The Mormons' rapid settlement in Utah brought immediate conflict with the Utes there, while the Colorado bands enjoyed a decade and a half of relative tranquility. Then, in 1863, in a treaty signed by leaders of only one or two tribes, the Colorado Utes were confined to a reservation. Though fairly large at first (some eighteen million acres), this reservation was quickly reduced in piecemeal fashion. In 1868, a second treaty limited Ute lands to the western third of Colorado. Scarcely five years later, as a response to demands from miners and entrepreneurs, a rich section of the reservation—some 3,500,000 acres of mineral lands in the San Juans—was excised in the Brunot Agreement. In none of these negotiations did all Ute tribes participate. Consequently, nonsigners felt no obligation to comply, and until 1880 several Ute tribes maintained their nomadic lifestyle—hunting where they pleased and ignoring reservation boundaries.[2]

Colorado's mineral boom in the late 1870s set in motion those events that eventually culminated in the wholesale removal of Utes from most of the region west of the Continental Divide and in the opening of that territory to white settlers. Mining towns emerged quickly at Leadville, Aspen, Tin Cup, Gothic, and elsewhere, while entrepôt towns sprang up at such places as Gunnison. Miners complained bitterly about the high cost of supplies packed in by mules or wagons. Even after the Denver and Rio Grande Railway was extended to Gunnnison in 1881, miners believed that foodstuffs could be produced much more cheaply in the undeveloped fertile valleys of the western slope.[3]

Sharing this belief were hundreds of newcomers who planned to take up land or plat the towns that would serve the farmers and ranchers. Many arrived with considerable information about the area, with some of it drawn from eyewitness accounts dating back to the eighteenth century. The earliest written descriptions came from Spanish missionaries, Fray Francisco Atanasio Domínguez and Fray Silvestre Vélez de Escalante, who traversed the region in 1776 while searching for a route connecting Santa Fe and California. Though they failed to reach California, they pioneered a major portion of what later became known as the Old Spanish Trail.[4] Their favorable descriptions were augmented in the early nineteenth century by an adventurer accompanying fur trader Antoine Roubidoux, who established posts at the junction of the Uncompahgre and Gunnison rivers and on the Uintah River (a tributary of the Green River in northeastern Utah). The adventurer, who journeyed with Roubidoux from Taos to the Uintah fort, extolled the "great abundance" of game, timber, and "rich valleys."[5]

More useful to prospective settlers were various reports prepared for the U.S. government, many of which were published. In 1853, Congress funded four surveys to find a suitable rail route to the Pacific. The "Central Route," Senator Thomas Hart Benton's favorite, would follow the thirty-eighth parallel to the Continental Divide and then proceed along western river valleys. Although thwarted in his attempt to have his son-in-law, John C. Frémont, named head of the survey, Benton convinced Edward F. Beale, newly appointed superintendent of Indian affairs for California, to use the proposed route when he went west in the early summer of 1853. Benton also raised money to send Frémont on a winter expedition along the route. The official survey, headed by Capt. John W. Gunnison, was sandwiched between these two expeditions. Printed accounts of all three expeditions were available by 1860. Although the Gunnison survey concluded that the Central Route was impractical, these expeditions demonstrated the possibility of travel on Colorado's western slope.[6]

Journals and dispatches of military personnel provided yet another source of information for would-be townbuilders and settlers. During the "Mormon War" of the late 1850s, both Capt. Randolph B. Marcy and Col. William W. Loring retraced portions of the earlier survey routes. In autumn 1857, Marcy set out from Fort Bridger, Wyoming, under orders "to cross the mountains by the most direct route to New Mexico." That route took his detachment along the Grand River to the Gunnison, where he then marched upstream.[7] The venture almost proved fatal. Because of heavy snow, Marcy's party lost the trail. After days without provisions, the soldiers began eating their mules. Nevertheless, they pushed on, and finally received aid from Fort Massachusetts, not far from Taos. Originating near Salt Lake City in midsummer 1858, Loring's expedition followed the same course, encountering several of Marcy's camps en route. Loring's trip was easier because of the season, and he and his party successfully crossed into the San Luis Valley via Cochetopa Pass, demonstrating the feasibility of wagon travel over the southern Rockies. Marcy's published memoir, describing his expedition, was widely read.[8]

Undoubtedly, the most valuable information available to prospective settlers consisted of the reports of Ferdinand V. Hayden's several expeditions for the U.S. Geographical and Geological Survey. For almost a decade, Hayden traversed the region west of the Rocky Mountains, and he foresaw the area's future. In 1873, Hayden sought funding to survey western Colorado because he believed that "the prospect of its rapid development within the next five years, by some of the most important railroads in the West, renders it very desirable that its resources be made known to the world at as early a date as possible."[9] Hayden's expeditions often included photographer William Henry Jackson, who provided the first photographs of Mesa Verde, Mount of the Holy Cross, and other less spectacular but nonetheless impressive western landscapes. In 1875, Jackson spent about a month on Colorado's western slope, and then he devoted the latter part of that year and early 1876 to preparing survey photographs for exhibition at the Centennial Exposition in Philadelphia;

the following year, the Hayden reports were published in atlas form. This *Atlas of Colorado* showed in magnificent detail not only the locations of rivers, valleys, and mountains, but also designated land suitable for agriculture, grazing, or mineral development.[10]

Thus, by the latter half of the 1870s, the availability of information about Colorado's western slope, the miners' demands for more and cheaper food supplies, and the desire of many others to farm the fertile river valleys led to demands from whites that "The Utes Must Go." The immediate excuse for removal was the Ute attack on the White River Agency in 1879. The killing of Nathan Meeker and the kidnapping of his family created a situation so volatile that in 1880 the Utes were forced to relinquish major portions of western Colorado. Under that arrangement, the White River Utes were exiled to Utah's Uintah Basin, the Southern Utes to the southwestern part of Colorado, and the Uncompahgre Utes to the confluence of the Gunnison and Grand Rivers—the Grand Valley. The land surrendered by the Indians was to be sold.[11]

The commissioners appointed to secure Ute signatures on the 1880 agreement were also empowered to select specific reservation sites. In the case of the Uncompahgre Utes, the commissioners decided that 150,000 acres of fertile land in the valley where the Gunnison flows into the Grand was "unsatisfactory," and what they deemed a more suitable location was designated in Utah. The Utes had no voice in the decision, and although they ultimately relocated, they did so reluctantly.[12]

It is hard not to read conspiracy into the commissioners' decision that the valley of the Grand was unfit for the support of some fourteen hundred Utes. Their decision left the area's legal status unclear. In the agreement of 1880, all lands surrendered by the Utes were to be sold, but the Grand Valley had not been formally relinquished by the Indians, nor was it part of a reservation. Land-hungry whites easily assumed that since the designation "Grand Valley" did not appear in the treaty, the area was part of the public domain and open for homesteading.[13] Two years later, they won the federal government to their point of view when Congress legitimatized all preemption claims for the Grand Valley as well as for some other parts of the Ute Reservation.[14]

For an "unsatisfactory" area, the Grand Valley quickly attracted settlers. For months, many whites had anticipated that the territory would be opened, and they had been gathering in the gateway town of Gunnison.[15] The manner in which so many went directly to the Grand Valley, passing up suitable agricultural and ranch land and potential townsites elsewhere, reflected the settlers' prior knowledge of the area. In August 1880 the agreement between the United States and the Utes was concluded, and on 1 September of the following year the last of the Uncompahgre Utes left western Colorado. Although the reservation was not to be officially open for another ten months, within days settlers began staking out farms, ranches, and townsites. Grand Junction was one of the towns.

1 · FORGING THE COMMUNITY
Town Builders and Family Men

"A better natural townsite . . . I have seldom seen."[1]

For months before the Utes surrendered Colorado's western slope in late summer 1881, prospective settlers gathered in Gunnison, at the edge of the reservation. Several had their sights set on the confluence of the Gunnison and Grand rivers. As soon as possible, these pioneers—virtually all male and unmarried—advanced to that point and initiated the building of a town. In subsequent months, some platted and incorporated the townsite, while others began businesses; together, they elected the town's first officials.

Pioneer town building in Grand Junction transpired at the hands of single men. Between 1881, when Grand Junction was nothing but sage brush and tumbleweeds, and 1900, when the town had elm-shaded streets, these settlers struggled to shape their community. Town building, moreover, occurred in concert with the formation of families, as the earliest pioneers married and as additional families immigrated. Thus, a key ingredient in Grand Junction's successful evolution was its familial environment.

At the time of the opening of the Ute Reservation, Gunnison was a bustling center. It formed the hub of a wheel whose rim stretched into the San Juans of southwestern Colorado, through the middle Rockies to Aspen, and into the San Luis Valley and the headwaters of the Rio Grande. Miners throughout the region obtained their supplies there. Two railroads, the Denver and Rio Grande and the Denver, South Park, and Pacific, furiously laid track in a race to reach the town.

Many of the people in Gunnison were speculators or would-be farmers, ranchers, and merchants awaiting the opening of the reservation. Among them was James W. Bucklin, a young attorney who had arrived in Colorado in 1877 with his University of Michigan law degree fresh in hand. He settled first in Denver, where he passed the Colorado bar exam and practiced for three years. His mind was elsewhere, however. Before moving to Colorado, he had visited the Centennial Exposition in Philadelphia and was perhaps inspired by William Henry Jackson's panorama of the territory west of the Continental Divide. As soon as he learned of the Utes' imminent removal, he determined to make his fortune in that attractive area. To be on hand when the reservation lands opened, he relocated in Gunnison in June 1880. In the eighteen months that he waited he practiced his craft, and during that time he made the acquaintance of Richard D. Mobley, another who saw future wealth in the western slope. Mobley had visited southwestern Colorado in 1877 or 1878, and like Bucklin, he planned to claim some of the Ute lands.[2]

Bucklin and Mobley were by no means the only men who viewed the mouth of the Gunnison as a potential townsite. George A. Crawford, no novice at town building, was also waiting for the opening of the reservation. In 1857, at the age of thirty, he had traveled by steamboat into Kansas Territory, where he helped to establish a town on the site of Fort Scott, a military post dating from the 1820s. Crawford was president of the Fort Scott Town Company, a position he held for twenty years. In the late 1860s, Crawford participated in the development of Osage Mission in central Kansas, and in 1876 he was secretary of the company that set up Short Creek in the Cherokee Strip of Oklahoma.

Crawford's building of communities was not limited to platting towns. In the years following the Civil War, he actively promoted immigration to Kansas, particularly in his capacity as associate editor of the *Kansas Farmer*. These activities drew the attention of national leaders, and in 1871 President Ulysses S. Grant named him to the planning commission for the Centennial Exposition in Philadelphia. While serving on that commission, Crawford learned about western Colorado from military personnel. William Henry Jackson's photographs may also have stimulated his interest.[3]

Crawford arrived in Gunnison in the early summer of 1881, dispatched by his half-brother Allison White, who wanted a report on his investments in the Gunnison Improvement Company. Crawford had intended to spend only a short period in Colorado, but once there he extended his stay, in large part because his health improved. During that time, he toured the region around Gunnison, often in the company of M. Rush Warner, general manager of the Gunnison Improvement Company. Crawford liked what he saw and changed his mind about returning to Kansas. Instead, he spent the remainder of the summer in planning his entry onto the Ute Reservation. He also renewed his acquaintanceship with R. D. Mobley, whom he had known in Kansas.[4]

Besides Crawford, Bucklin, and Mobley, there were others interested in the choice real estate at the junction of the Gunnison and the Grand rivers. Four young civilians who had worked as teamsters for the military post at the Uncompahgre cantonment were the first claimants to the site. William McGinley, J. Clayton Nichols, and O. D. and Milton Russell had twice tried to enter the reservation before the Ute removal, only to be arrested by the military and returned to the post. On a third attempt in early September 1881, they contrived their way into the Grand Valley and discovered that the Indians had vacated the area. They quickly staked out ranches and returned to Gunnison to file their claims.

When McGinley, Nichols, and the Russell brothers arrived in Gunnison with the news that the Indians had left the territory, Crawford decided to enter the still officially closed reservation and establish claims of his own. On 17 September, he, Rush Warner, and two others departed, led by McGinley and Nichols.[5] They stopped at the mouth of the Uncompaghre River, where Crawford staked out a town, naming it after that river. There, he was overtaken by Mobley (Bucklin lay ill in Gunnison, unable to participate in the entry), who also had moved onto the reservation when he heard that the Utes had gone. Mobley camped with Crawford's party, and Crawford convinced him to join forces.[6] The new team now traveled the rest of the way down the Gunnison River to its confluence with the Grand. There, on 26 September they staked their claim. Crawford pithily summarized that day in his diary: "Hunt for town site. Select Sec. 14. T.1. S.R.1.W."[7] The area did not appear attractive to the eye, but the men believed that its future potential was enormous.

> The cotton wood trees fringed the river bottom, the sage brush covered the valley from one end to the other. Not a tree, not a house, not a drop of water, not a green thing

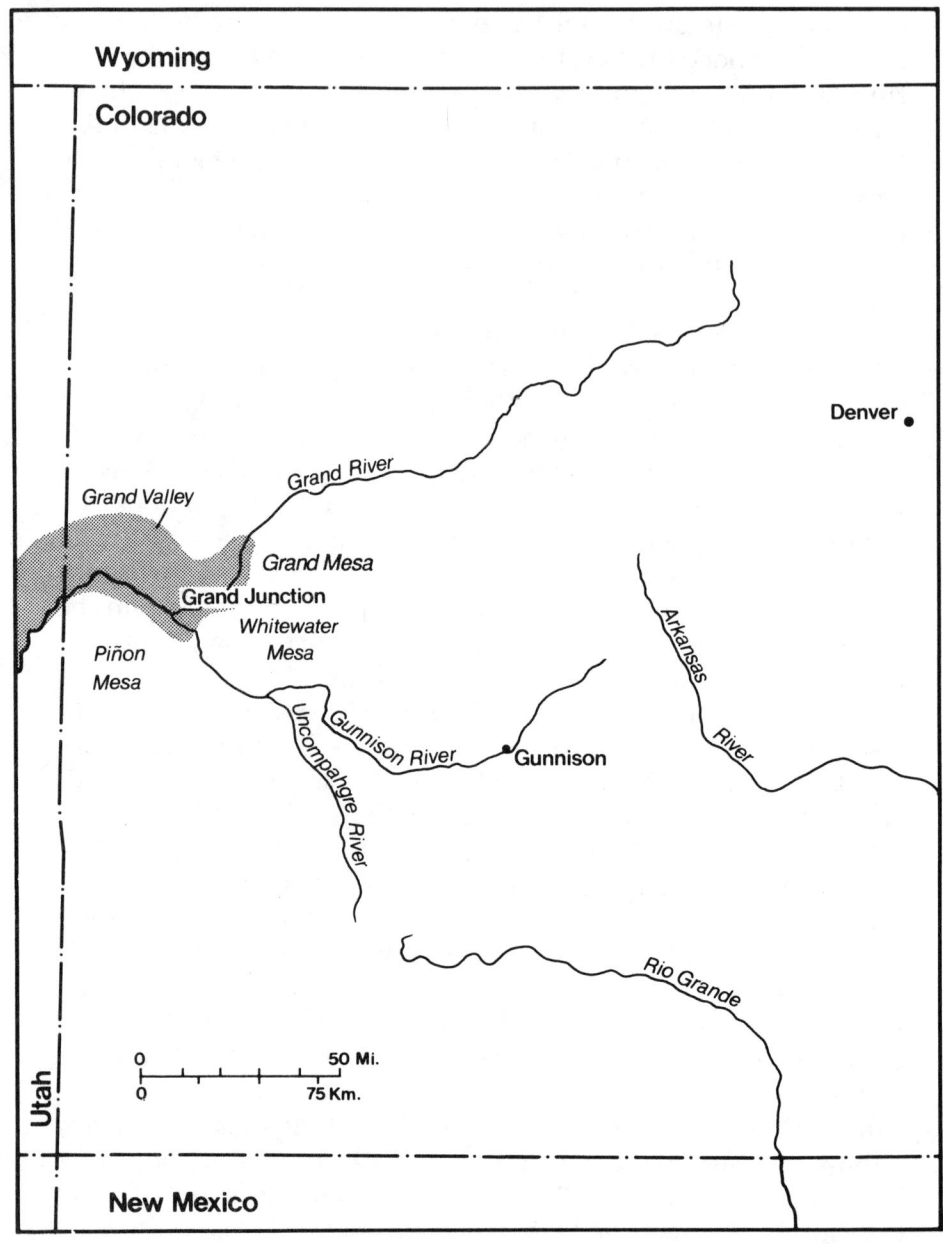

Colorado's Western Slope

dotted the valley. . . . Nothing but a barren waste. And yet, there was something in it which, at once, appealed to the senses, and told one that this would one day be a most fruitful and luxuriant valley.[8]

Once the site was determined, matters moved along rapidly. Crawford's town-building experience proved invaluable. He hired McGinley and Nichols to build cabins on each quarter section in order to secure the claim. With Mobley, he immediately returned to Gunnison to register the claim to the townsite. Then he, Mobley, and Bucklin formally incorporated the Grand Junction Town Company on 10 October 1881. Initially, there were six shareholders: Crawford, Mobley, Bucklin, Warner, and two Philadelphia investors: Crawford's half-brother, Allison White, and H. E. Rood. Later, these shares were reduced when Crawford's backers began to shoulder more of the financial responsibility and when the Denver and Rio Grande Railway received half the town company's stock in exchange for a promise to locate several of its operations in Grand Junction.

During that first autumn and winter, Crawford and his associates tackled other tasks that they considered essential to Grand Junction's generation. The first was to ensure the construction of a post office, which they requested in November. Their subsequent activities followed the traditional "planned community" pattern detailed by historian John Reps:

> The tract was then surveyed into streets, blocks, lots and open spaces. Only after this initial design was determined were houses, shops, mills, churches, stores, and public buildings erected on predetermined locations.[9]

In March of 1882, George Crawford, now president of the Grand Junction Town Company, approved Grand Junction's "initial design"; James Bucklin notarized it, and together they filed with the county clerk in Gunnison.[10] The town company's officers laid out the town in a typical grid fashion, with streets north–south and east–west. They numbered the north–south streets "First" through "Twelfth," and assigned names to the east–west avenues. With First and Twelfth, "North" and "South" formed the town's boundaries. Later, Grand Junction would grow as speculators laid out additions to the original site.[11] Town officers named one avenue for Ouray, a

Ute chief, another for his wife Chipeta, and a third for the tribe. They also named avenues for H. E. Rood and Allison White, the Philadelphia investors.

The officers did more than set out lots and provide street names. They had greater expectations for their town: it would contain parks, schools, churches, and would be a seat of government. Accordingly, they allotted four city blocks for parks and another for "Central High School." They earmarked corners of four blocks for elementary schools and a fifth corner for the city infirmary, and they allocated the southwest corners in six blocks of White Avenue for churches. Finally, they set aside a full block for city and county buildings—a bit premature as Grand Junction would not be named county seat for another year, but indicative of expectations. Moreover, though they democratically set aside park space in each quarter of the town, they clearly thought that certain areas would be more likely to house the well-to-do. Main Street and Grand and Gunnison avenues were wider than other streets, and the lots facing those streets were deeper than most residential lots. Seventh Street was a boulevard, with space for trees in the center, and it was the only street whose lots faced east–west rather than north–south. And, in harmony with the town officials' plan, the homes on Main, Grand, Gunnison, and especially Seventh streets were larger and housed the more affluent.[12]

In June 1882, when the Ute Reservation was officially opened for settlement, town company officers encouraged settlers to incorporate the town of Grand Junction, and thirty-three voters unanimously agreed. (Colorado statutes required thirty qualified electors for town incorporation). The following month, residents elected the first mayor and aldermen. The town company paid the mayor's expenses to the federal land office at Leadville, where the mayor filed incorporation papers for the town.

Crawford's Kansas town-building experience had also taught him the importance of a local newspaper. Its major function was to advertise the new community to outsiders, but it also helped to keep residents informed and entertained. In September 1882, he and Bucklin traveled to Denver, hoping to encourage someone with newspaper expertise to locate in Grand Junction. The most likely candidate was William E. Pabor, a man already interested in the western slope and who had been corresponding with Crawford. Pabor was editor of the *Colorado Farmer* and a vigorous promoter of the state, who later published two books aimed at attracting immigrants: *Colorado as an Agricultural State* (1883) and *The Fruit Culture of Colorado* (1883). Though Pabor subsequently moved to the Grand Valley, he did not publish Grand Junction's newspaper; instead, Edwin Price, a friend of Bucklin's, undertook that enterprise.[13]

Bucklin knew Price from his days in Denver, and was impressed with the man's editorial skills. Crawford was equally impressed, and Price was eager to begin anew in Grand Junction. "Within two weeks' time," Price remembered, "I was on my way west with a complete printing outfit." Rail transportation stopped forty miles short of Grand Junction, and Price had to travel the remainder of the way by wagon. Those forty miles, he later recalled, were the

> roughest and most uncomfortable journey I have ever made. Over the dry, barren, adobe and rocky foothills, was the rockiest road imaginable. It was the dreariest landscape I had ever seen. . . . I was ready to sell out for thirty cents.

Once the stage had crested "Orchard Mesa" and the Grand Valley came into view, Price's

> misgivings gave way to joy and hope. A few miles down the valley [I] saw the walls of new buildings in the course of construction and evidence of civilization. My courage came back, and as we crossed the river on the ferry-boat, landing us on the Grand Valley Soil, I became reconciled.[14]

Price lost no time in setting up his business. Within two weeks, the first issue of the *Grand Junction News* rolled off the press.

While the officers of the company were busy in endowing Grand Junction with the accoutrements of a town—post office, plat, incorporation, and newspaper—other people began to form what would be the community's economic and social structure. Within four years of the Ute removal, Grand Junction was a thriving pioneer settlement of more than 850. It had about seventy businesses, five churches, and a dozen voluntary associations. But who were these new inhabitants? Like most people in the West, including James Bucklin, they were native-born, unmarried males in their twenties and early thirties who were looking for a likely place to begin their careers.[15] Charles E. Mitchell, for example, was twenty-three and single when he settled in Grand Junction. Mitchell was born in Vermont, and learned engineering at the state university. He then moved west, and was a member of the government survey team that measured the Grand Valley in January 1881. Mitchell apparently liked what he saw, for he returned later that year as the owner of the first grocery store in Grand Junction. Like Mitchell, Charles McCarey was single when he moved to the Grand Valley. McCarey had grown up in Colorado, migrating there from Virginia with his parents when he was twelve. Ten years later, in 1884, he left Denver for the western slope, working first on the Grand Valley (irrigation) Ditch and then settling in Fruita, a town about ten miles west of Grand Junction, where that town company promised him a lot if he operated a blacksmith shop for six months. At the end of that period, he sold out and moved to Grand Junction, where he believed that his chances were better of making a good living from smithing.

Bucklin, Mitchell, and McCarey typify the pioneer community's first settlers, four-fifths of whom were native born. In 1885, the median age of Grand Junction's population was 27. Males tended to be older (29.5) than females (22.6), with—as Figure 1 demonstrates—the largest percentage of males clustered in the age group 30 to 34. Grand Junction's demographic composition reveals a heavy preponderance of males and an overall ratio of 147 males to 100 females. For those old enough to marry—that is, those of age 15 or older—the ratio was even more lopsided: 161 to 100.[16] Because of the uneven sex ratio, more men of marriageable age were single than wed, as Table 1 demonstrates: 56.8 percent were single, 35.8 percent were married, and 7.4 percent were widowed or divorced. The pattern, however, was very different for women and men: most adult women (61.0 percent) were married, while most adult men were single. The ratio of unmarried men to unmarried women obviously meant that not all men could begin families, since there were five men of marriageable age for every two women.

There were, of course, married men in the pioneer settlement: about one in three men had spouses when they moved to Grand Junction. Some, like Edwin Price, were in their early twenties and virtually newlyweds. Price came to the settlement in October 1882, and his wife Lola joined him a month later, arriving on the first train into Grand Junction. They had been married for a year and a month. Most of the married men and women, however, were older than the Prices and had children. For example, J. H. and Ella Belle Ackerman

FORGING THE COMMUNITY

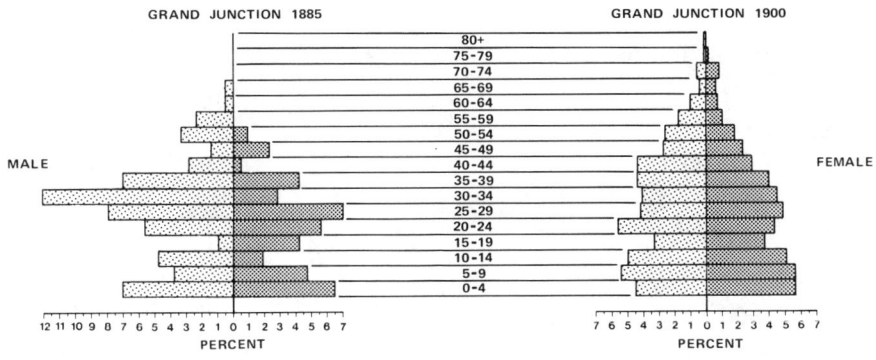

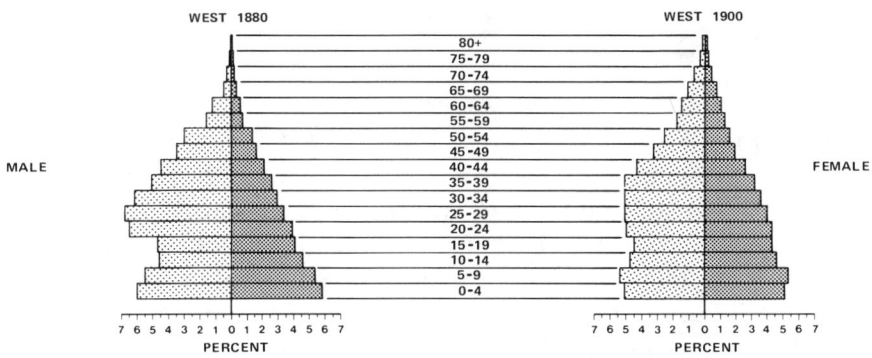

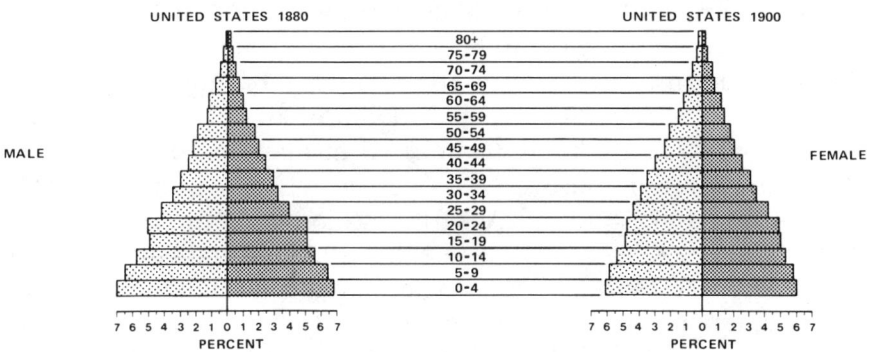

FIGURE 1: Population Distribution for Grand Junction, the West, and the United States

Table 1
Marital Status of the Population, Age 15 and Over

	All Adults	Female	Male
A. 1885			
single	47.4%	32.2%	56.8%
married	45.5	61.0	35.8
widowed/divorced	7.1	6.8	7.4
N	154	59	95
B. 1900			
single	31.8	23.6	39.0
married	58.5	63.1	54.3
widowed/divorced	9.7	13.1	6.6
N	597	282	315

arrived in Grand Junction in the spring of 1883 with their five-year-old son Harry and two-year-old daughter Alice. They had moved frequently before settling in Grand Junction. Born in Paterson, New Jersey, J. H. Ackerman evidently moved to Illinois, where he met and married Ella Belle some time in the early 1870s. In 1878 they were in Texas, where Harry was born, and by 1881 they had relocated to Colorado.[17] J. H. was a partner in a construction business, which had enough work to employ two dozen men in the pioneer settlement.

Grand Junction's 1885 population resided in 322 households, and slightly more than half contained no conjugal units or children, as Table 2 demonstrates. Instead, they consisted of single persons, and in almost all cases, these were males living alone or with other adults. Simple family households (comprised of married couples with or without children) constituted 41 percent of the community. Most such households, like the Ackermans, contained married couples with children, although some, like that of Edwin and Lola Price, had no children and others were single-parent households. Most were quite also small: the mean household size was 2.5. Only a third (36.0 percent) contained children, and even fewer—12.8 percent—included any relatives. Except for hotels and boardinghouses, very few households included lodgers and boarders (4.0 percent) or servants (3.4 percent).[18]

Grand Junction's demographic profile shifted drastically after

Table 2
Household Structure and Composition,
1885 and 1900

	1885	1900
A. Household Structure		
Mean number of children	.8	1.6
Structure		
solitary	46.7%	13.2%
no family	3.6	4.2
simple family	41.1	69.8
extended	8.4	9.3
multiple	0.0	2.6
indeterminate	0.0	.9
B. Household Composition		
Mean household size*	2.5	3.9
Percent households with		
child	36.0%	66.4%
parent	3.1	5.5
sibling	5.0	5.2
other relative	4.7	6.7
lodgers/boarders	4.0	13.1
servants	3.4	4.4
others	2.5	3.6
N	322	900

*Excluding boardinghouses.

1885. The age structure changed, as did the sex ratio of the community, and the foreign-born proportion of the population declined. The population was more evenly dispersed in 1900 than it had been in 1885, with both more youngsters and more elderly people. So many more younger people resided in the town that the median age fell to 25. Age differences between women and men were also reduced: for women, the median age was 24.1 and for men, 25.9. By the turn of the century, there were almost as many females as males in the town. The sex ratio had declined to 104:100. The community's demographic profile came to resemble the traditional pyramid shape that is associated with stable populations. A comparison of the population pyramids (Figure 1) vividly demonstrates Grand Junction's changed sex ratios and age structures.

Marriage patterns were also modified as Grand Junction matured. As a result of the changed sex ratios, the number of married persons increased. Table 1 reveals that among those persons old enough to wed, more than half were married (58.5 percent), about a third single (31.8 percent), and the rest widowed or divorced. The percentage of married females remained constant, but by 1900 more than half the men were wed.

A few of the married couples who initially settled in pioneer Grand Junction remained to build the community. Editor Edwin Price and his wife stayed, and their daughter Lola Eudora was the first child born in Grand Junction. J. H. and Ella Belle Ackerman also decided that Grand Junction was the place to raise their family, which by the end of the century included four more children. Moreover, the families that remained were bolstered by the continued settlement of other families. By 1900, Grand Junction contained at least five hundred families that bought property and joined local organizations.

Grand Junction's development also encouraged the creation of new families. Virtually all of the single people who remained after 1885 eventually married, as did some of the widows and widowers and the divorced. James Bucklin, in fact, married twice after settling in Grand Junction. His first union with Maggie Champion was short-lived; only a year after their marriage in 1884, Maggie died in childbirth. Bucklin's loss multiplied when his twin sons succumbed within weeks of their mother. He remained a widower for a decade, and in 1895, he married Mary Lapham. Like Bucklin, both Charles McCarey and Charles Mitchell also began families. In 1886, McCarey married Nettie Covey, a young woman he had known while growing up in Denver; and two years earlier, Mitchell had wed Esther Kent (or "Bessie," as she preferred). Bessie and her sister Emma had arrived in Grand Junction in 1883, and like other single women in the pioneer community, both were popular. When Emma wed Addison J. McCune five years later, the bachelors of Grand Junction lamented their loss in the newspaper. This was McCune's third marriage. He had grown up in Ohio and at age nineteen, in 1870, had moved to Colorado for his health. There, he worked as a surveyor for various railroad and canal companies before going to Grand Junction in 1883 to conduct the survey for the Grand Valley Ditch. He decided to become a resident. McCune was a widower in 1885, but he was not alone. His nine-year-old daughter Stella and his sister

Julia resided with him. He also took in boarders and had a school teacher staying in his household in 1885. The following year, McCune married his boarder, Maggie Owens, but that union soon collapsed.

The married proportion of the community also increased as youngsters who grew up in Grand Junction began their own families. George Fletcher and his sister Ollie were children when their parents established a hotel and one of the four boarding houses in the pioneer community. Like the Ackermans, the Fletchers relocated several times before settling permanently in Grand Junction. Fletcher was born in Pennsylvania in 1844 and moved to Illinois sometime during his youth. There, at the age of twenty, in 1867, he married Ellen Feltman. A year later, their first child, George, was born. The Fletcher family then moved to Kansas, where a daughter, Ollie, was born in 1871, followed three years latter by twin boys, Archer and Alvan. In 1882, they moved to Grand Junction and opened their hotel. Three years later, they had seventeen boarders residing with them, a sign that business was good. The Fletcher family remained in Grand Junction, where Ellen and Robert saw their children reach maturity. In 1891 Ollie married, and George also wed four years later.

The formation of new families among Grand Junction's pioneers as well as the arrival of additional families transformed the community's residential patterns. In 1885 more than half the town's population resided in households without a family unit; by 1900 fewer than a fifth did. Instead, as Table 2 illustrates, most persons (69.8 percent) now lived in simple family households. In a few instances, more than one family shared a household (2.6 percent), with some married children living with their parents.

The formation of families also had an impact on household composition. Over the fifteen-year period between 1885 and 1900, household size increased (the mean household size was now 3.9), and the proportion of households with children doubled, from one in three in 1885 to two in three by 1900. Clearly, the youthfulness of the adult population—many of whom had recently married and were still very much in their childbearing years—contributed to the increased proportion of households with children. This phenomenon may be observed in the Price household, where five children were present in 1900; in the McCarey household, with two sons; and in the Bucklin household, with one son. Even the next generation had started families. Ollie Fletcher Boyer had two daughters, and her brother George and his wife had one. The increase in the number of families, moreover, altered the living arrangements for unmarried people. By the turn of the century, many single women and men chose to board or lodge in family settings rather than in the large boardinghouses present in the pioneer settlement. Sometimes, couples without children also boarded.

In its pioneer phase, then, Grand Junction's demographic profile conformed generally to that of the area west of the one-hundreth meridian, where, until the mid-twentieth century, people were older than in the United States as a whole (and older than in any other region of the country); and that difference was greater during the periods of early settlement. Median age in 1870 for the West was 24.2; for the country, 20.2. That region has been also distinguished by a predominance of males. While the sex ratio was about even in the country at large, there were 247 males for every 100 females in the West in 1870. The West had a disproportionate share of foreign-born people during the height of its mineral booms. According to the 1870 census, about one person in three living in the Mountain and Pacific areas was foreign born.

As the West became more settled, its exaggerated demographic configuration modified, but did not yet conform to the nation at large. By 1890, median age increased to 25.2 (the national median was 22.1). The ratio of men to women steadily declined, but even at the turn of the century it was 128:100. Uneven sex ratios meant that not all adults could marry and have families; as a result, the West has also had fewer children, a characteristic not shared by earlier frontiers. The foreign-born proportion also decreased as more native-born people responded to perceived opportunities in the West.[19]

Like the West, Grand Junction's pioneer population tended to be older (the median age was twenty-nine), and its sex ratio in 1885 was typical of a western frontier (147:100). On the other hand, there were many more native-born people in the community than in the region in general. Over time, Grand Junction's demographic profile also became less exaggerated. By 1900, the median age dropped to twenty-five, an age roughly the same as the median age in the region but still several years older than in the nation. The town continued to include an extremely high percentage of the native born (especially for a town with so many railroad workers). Most startling, however, was its changed sex ratio. Now, women almost equaled men in the town.

Whether the pattern of an older, more native-born population observed for early Grand Junction was unique or common to pioneer communities is difficult to determine because most studies concerned with the connection between demographic change and the frontier have focused on periods occurring several years (and sometimes decades) after initial settlement.[20] Equally problematic is the fact that almost all of these studies rely on county-level data, data that absorb towns, yet the urban environment helps explain Grand Junction's changed demographic composition in 1900—in particular, the increased presence of women. The tendency to utilize county-level data is all the more surprising because the urban nature of the frontier experience is well known.[21]

If the Grand Junction experience was duplicated in other towns on the frontier, then those persons attracted to towns tended to be older and more likely to be native born than those moving to the rural countryside.[22] Moreover, a society dominated by males, which is traditionally associated with cattle towns and mining settlements, may, in fact, be characteristic of the early stages in all towns and cities.[23]

Between its initial settlement in 1881 and 1900 Grand Junction experienced sweeping demographic changes. The early community had been characterized by a predominance of single males in their early thirties who lived alone or in boardinghouses; by 1900, the sex ratio was almost equal and more adults were wed than single. Moreover, almost everyone, regardless of marital status, resided in private homes. The continued influx of families and the formation of new families promoted these changes. Not only were more people married in 1900, and therefore residing in family settings, but single persons also lived with families. The influence of family was not limited to living arrangements, however. As the following chapters illustrate, the family played a decisive role in shaping the society of the pioneer settlement, and later, the small town of Grand Junction.

2 · WEAVING THE ECONOMIC FABRIC

"The city of the future...."[1]

In late November 1881, George A. Crawford wrote to officials of the Denver and Rio Grande Railway portraying Grand Junction as "the city of the future of the Grand River." "A better natural townsite than the one we have chosen," he continued, "I have seldom seen." Crawford's assessment of Grand Junction as a "natural town site" was not exaggerated; it possessed several features that made it attractive to pioneers and town builders alike. Located at the confluence of the Grand and Gunnison rivers, it would have ample water for irrigation, while the nearby river valleys represented the most likely routes for both roads and railways. The 1853 railroad survey across the western slope had followed the Gunnison to the Grand, as would the Denver and Rio Grande Railway in 1882. (Grand Junction later became a railroad as well as a river "junction" when a rail line was completed connecting Grand Junction with Glenwood Springs, Red Cliff, and Aspen and its silver mines.) Once the Denver and Rio Grande arrived, Grand Junction became an entrepôt, providing goods and services for the Grand Valley. When the town was designated as the seat for Mesa County in 1883, the community's regional preeminence multiplied.[2]

Grand Junction would become the dominant town in an economic and political hierarchy on the western slope that emerged within a decade after its founding and which remains relatively intact to the present day. However, that dominance was not realized without competition. The strongest competition came from towns that serviced mining in western Colorado, particularly Durango, Gunnison, and Aspen. Established in the summer of 1880, Durango grew to a population of twenty-five hundred by the end of the year. Its economy also diversified quickly: In addition to providing supplies to miners in the San Juans and to ranchers and farmers in the Animas Valley, Durango's smelting facilities increased its regional importance. Gunnison similarly provided goods and services to miners. In the late 1870s and early 1880s, that community thrived, in large part because of the railroad, and it served as a jumping-off point for western-slope settlers.

The largest and most sophisticated town on the western slope, however, was Aspen. Mining in the Roaring Fork Valley began in the late 1870s, and by 1882 Aspen had several smelters, although a rail line was not completed until 1887. In 1890, Aspen's population was about five thousand, and it had all the amenities of a small city, including stores, schools, and an opera. At times as many as a dozen newspapers kept the residents informed.[3] The Panic of 1893, however, marked the turning point in Aspen's dominance. Although ore production remained high for another fifteen years, the boom was over, and after the mid-1890s, Aspen's population declined precipitously. The economic distress of 1893 was not limited to mining towns, although such places were the hardest to be hit. Shipping and service centers also faced business failures and economic pressures. As the price of silver dropped, railroads were forced into receivership, and banks failed. Only unemployment soared.[4]

Grand Junction emerged from the depression in a stronger position than many western slope communities—in large part because the Denver and Rio Grande Railway remained sound.[5] Although several towns had been laid out on the recently opened Ute Reservation, by 1900 Grand Junction had become (and still remains) the largest town in the region. The town developed as a service center to farmers, and it generated capital through its exports, chiefly fruit. The foresight of its town founders facilitated Grand Junction's ascendancy. They platted the community at a strategic point, the confluence of the Grand and the Gunnison. More importantly, they enticed the Denver and Rio Grande Railway to invest in the community's future.

Others, besides the officers of the town company, moved into the area recognizing the advantages of locating at the junction of the Grand and the Gunnison. By the following summer of 1882, several pioneers had established businesses. In subsequent years, these firms and the Grand Junction Town Company vigorously promoted the municipality. In addition, other settlers, though not as visibly active in economic ventures, also participated in the community. While they may not have had as much to gain by Grand Junction's growth and development, they had to earn a living and they supported many of the aims of the town company and the independent entrepreneurs. Moreover, the relationship between the company and the pioneers was complementary. Both played a part in Grand Junction's success: To turn a profit, the Grand Junction Town Company had to attract settlers; at the same time, the organizational activities of the company freed settlers to pursue their own ventures.

The company's primary goal was to show a profit by promoting the town and selling lots. It also participated directly in the town's economic life by becoming a major source of employment, especially in the construction trades. The company built the first hotel, started a brick factory, and constructed a canal (the Pacific Slope Ditch) to furnish water to the town. These endeavors provided jobs and attracted settlers. Among the most far-reaching actions of the company were the negotiations with the Denver and Rio Grande Railway.

George Crawford, a self-described "old town builder," recognized the vital role that a railroad would play in Grand Junction's future. He began his campaign with John A. McMurtrie, chief engineer for the Denver and Rio Grande.

> So whilst your Co. is doing so much[,] we try to do a little for the country. But we can't do it without [the Denver and Rio Grande's] co-operation. . . . I wish to work with your folks, to act advisedly with you, and in no way to trespass upon any of their fields of operation. Now what I am anxious about at present is to have your line located on our side of the river and through our town site or on the border.[6]

Whether or not the Denver and Rio Grande's officials shared Crawford's enthusiasm for Grand Junction's future, they did locate a depot in the community, to the great relief of settlers and town builders alike.[7] To whet McMurtrie's interest, Crawford mentioned coal deposits in the area, asking in a postscript: "Have you made your arrangements for ties, bridge timber &c. I have parties on look out for timber."[8] Crawford also wrote to David C. Dodge, general manager of the Denver and Rio Grande, freely acknowledging the railroad's importance to Grand Junction's development: "[I] came here to locate the future city of the Grand River country—the D. & R. G. consenting, of course."⁹ Dodge forwarded Crawford's letter (as well as the one sent to McMurtrie) to Robert F. Weitbrec, manager of construction.

> Herewith I send you a couple of letters from Crawford, supposed to be a townsite man. What have you done about locations of Stations on the Utah line? While I think it is well to work with outside parties in these matters, I don't believe they are entitled to all the cream.

Weitbrec replied that he had done "nothing definite yet" because "no titles can be secured . . . until the reservation is thrown open for settlement . . ." (and that would not be done for another six months). He added: "[t]hen the first man at the Land Office is the best man." Concerned about "squatters," Dodge now had second thoughts.

> Will it not be better to "go in" with the Squatters, as they are bound to have some way to protect themselves at the Land Office when the land is for sale. It seems to me it will be better to let them pay all the expense, and give us 1/3d or 1/2 interest free of cost.

Weitbrec agreed, asking, "If they will do so, yes. Shall I go ahead on that basis?" Dodge answered in the affirmative, and Grand Junction became a station on the Utah line.¹⁰

But the Denver and Rio Grande's interest in Grand Junction did not end with the agreement to build a depot. Crawford remained in contact with company officials, and in July 1882, the town company and the railroad struck a bargain. In exchange for half the stock in the Grand Junction Town Company, the Denver and Rio Grande agreed to locate its maintenance shops and roundhouse in Grand Junction. More importantly, the Denver and Rio Grande promised that when it completed its line down the Grand River from Red Cliff, Grand Junction would be divisional headquarters. Finally, the Denver and Rio Grande pledged to "foster and encourage the growth and development of . . . Grand Junction." Then, the town company's board of directors was reconstructed to reflect the railroad's increased influence. Half the directors were now executives of the Denver and Rio Grande.¹¹

As a result of Crawford's promotion and the Denver and Rio

Grande's action, Grand Junction became the principal rail center between Pueblo, Colorado, and Salt Lake City, Utah. Heralded by the *Grand Junction News* as "our army of relief," the railroad arrived in November 1882 and became a major booster of town growth, contributing directly by bringing in settlers, exporting produce, and providing jobs.[12] Within a year, "work was so far advanced on the main [railway] building that . . . the storeroom supplies were removed from Gunnison and established at [the Grand Junction] station."[13]

Although the railroad and the Grand Junction Town Company played major roles in the economic life of the new community, they were not the only businesses to make an appearance during the first year. No store of any sort existed until Charles Mitchell brought in the first provisions in early December 1881. He had a general store in operation by Christmas. At about the same time, a saloon also opened, which undoubtedly made the holidays a bit more lively. Seven months later, when Grand Junction was formally incorporated, the town included four general stores, seven saloons, three hotels and restaurants, two blacksmiths, a meat market, a pharmacy, five brick factories, and a sawmill (not located in the town, but providing lumber for its building). In addition, two lawyers and a doctor had taken up resident in the town.[14]

Business activity tended to be somewhat erratic over short intervals, but two patterns clearly emerged during the first two decades. First, as Grand Junction secured its position on the western slope, there was a relatively steady numerical increase in the business community. During the town's early years, the expansion came in such fundamental enterprises as groceries and saloons; later years witnessed more specialized stores. Second, as Grand Junction became intertwined in regional and national economies, the proportion of independent operators declined, and the number of managers and agents representing companies with corporate headquarters outside the town multiplied.[15]

The number of businesses swelled in Grand Junction's first two decades. In 1883, a state business directory listed 59 commercial enterprises in the settlement; by 1900 that number had tripled to 181. Population increase and improved transportation explain this growth. As more people settled in Grand Junction and homesteaded the surrounding countryside, new businesses emerged to meet the demand. Improved transportation also fostered the growth of the business community. The railroad made it possible for stores to handle a variety of goods.[16] In addition, as roads were built to connect the town to outlying farms, ranches, and other communities, Grand Junction consolidated command over its hinterland. For example, when the Roan Creek Toll Road to Glenwood Springs was completed in 1886, two local companies immediately established stage service.[17]

The initial advantage, which Grand Junction enjoyed as a result of the Grand Junction Town Company's actions, operated to stabilize the business community as well, and by the early 1890s most of the first businesses were so firmly established that few competitors emerged, and those that did seldom survived.[18] The ability of existing merchants to accommodate increased population did not mean, however, that economic opportunity in business was closed. Instead, in the early 1890s, successful new stores tended to be of the specialized variety.

From the outset there had been specialty stores in Grand Junction, but most failed, particularly in the first decade. For example, such shops as "ladies bazaar" or "gents furnishings" never lasted for more than a year or two, although many stores of this type were opened during the period. More surprising than its failure was the opening of a store specializing in "Chinese goods" in 1891, since there were only two or three Chinese in the town. One early specialty business that succeeded was photography. In 1884, T. E. Barnhouse opened his photography studio and apparently had a large enough clientele to remain in operation. In 1891, he took in a partner, S. N. Wheeler, who subsequently bought him out and was still in business at the turn of the century. Other photographers arrived in Grand Junction, but none remained for very long. Townspeople believed that a photographic record of family and community activities was necessary, but not until the late 1890s was the level of business large enough to support more than one photographer.

The relative decline in the number of independent businessmen in Grand Junction provides another measure of changed economic opportunity. In the town's earlier years, local entrepreneurs owned their businesses. Of the 59 firms in 1883, none was identified with a national company. In 1885, Western Union became the first outside firm to employ an agent in Grand Junction. By the early 1890s other outside enterprises had offices in the town. Branches of such national firms as Wells Fargo Express, Singer Sewing Machine, and Continental Oil had opened. At the same time, locally chartered fruit and produce organizations sought to export the area's crops. All of them established local managerial structures, creating in Grand Junction a group of men who did not own businesses, as had been the case in the earlier settlement, but who nevertheless contributed significantly to the town's financial activity. In Grand Junction's pioneer settlement, the people who owned the businesses lived in the community. By 1900, about 7 percent of the people listed in the Grand Junction section of the state business directory were agents for outside companies.

Although the number of businesses in Grand Junction tripled between 1883 and 1900, businessmen by no means dominated the economic framework. Indeed, the proportion of the population involved in business increased very little—from 13.7 percent in 1885 to 16.0 percent in 1900. While the percentage of businessmen remained constant, other occupations experienced variation, and some of it was considerable. In general, the opportunity for workers remained high; certain sectors of the economy, however, decreased in relative importance as the town developed.

During the early years, construction jobs were the most plentiful as pioneers built cabins, worked on the first hotel, and erected structures for the railroad. For example, J. H. Ackerman and his partner, J. J. Lumsden, had as much work as they could handle and provided "constant employment" for about twenty-five men.[19] Necessary materials were close at hand. Piñon Mesa, a low plateau west of the town, supplied timber for construction and jobs for lumbermen. Clay was plentiful, and by autumn 1882, several kilns fired bricks for building materials as well as furnishing another source of employment.[20] The Denver and Rio Grande Railway purchased large quantities of brick to build the Grand Junction roundhouse, depot, and other facilities. In addition, the railroad needed brick to erect various buildings at other places along the "Utah line."

The railroad not only furnished employment; it also encouraged the development of service-oriented occupations to meet the needs of the primarily single male work force: boarding and laundry facilities, barber shops, and, especially in the first year or two, prostitutes. Editor Edwin Price later remembered the "unusual number of 'sporting ladies' " and saloons. "On [their] account," Price recalled, "[Colorado Avenue] had gained the name of 'Hoodoo Ave.' where many drunken quarrels and shooting scraps took place." However, railroad workers contributed more than their unpleasant social behavior to the fledgling community, for they also cashed their paychecks in Grand Junction. Moreover, once the line to Salt Lake was completed, railroad laborers left, taking their "companions" with them. The imprint of "Hoodoo Ave." was nevertheless established, and the area concerned residents for years.[21]

In these first years, the physical needs of the countryside defined the occupational structure. Most men were involved in constructing buildings and homes, in working for the railroad, or in developing the agricultural hinterland. Figure 2 displays the relative importance of various occupations in the pioneer settlement.[22] Artisans comprised slightly more than one-fifth of the occupational force, and another one-fifth were in transportation and communication. Carpenters made up the largest single skilled craft. In all, building trades accounted for more than one-third of the artisans. Railroad-related occupations dominated the transportation and communication category, and half of those persons who reported railroad occupations were laborers. Agriculture, personal service, and business pursuits accounted for about 14 percent each.[23]

By 1900 the occupational structure had greatly expanded. Artisans and persons involved in transportation and communication grew, and as Figure 2 illustrates, they maintained their relative importance in Grand Junction's occupational scheme. The commercial side of the town now provided more occupational opportunity, as measured by the increase in sales personnel and the growing managerial sector. Finally, the proportion of persons classified as general laborers almost doubled.[24] A sign of the growing separation between the town and its countryside was the relative decline in the proportion of inhabitants who considered themselves to be farmers or ranchers.

Skilled workers in increasing numbers found employment in Grand Junction, and by the turn of the century they comprised more than half of those employed.[25] In the 1885 enumeration, artisans made up 21.6 percent of the gainfully employed; by 1900 that percentage had grown to 26.9 percent. Similarly, the number of people involved in transportation and communication had increased from 20.6 percent to 24.3 percent. These findings point out the importance of studying occupational opportunity within the community's economic framework.[26] Unlike many frontier towns, Grand Junction succeeded in securing its position in the economic hierarchy of the western slope (to the dismay of other towns), and thus provided opportunities for skilled and unskilled workers. For Grand Junction,

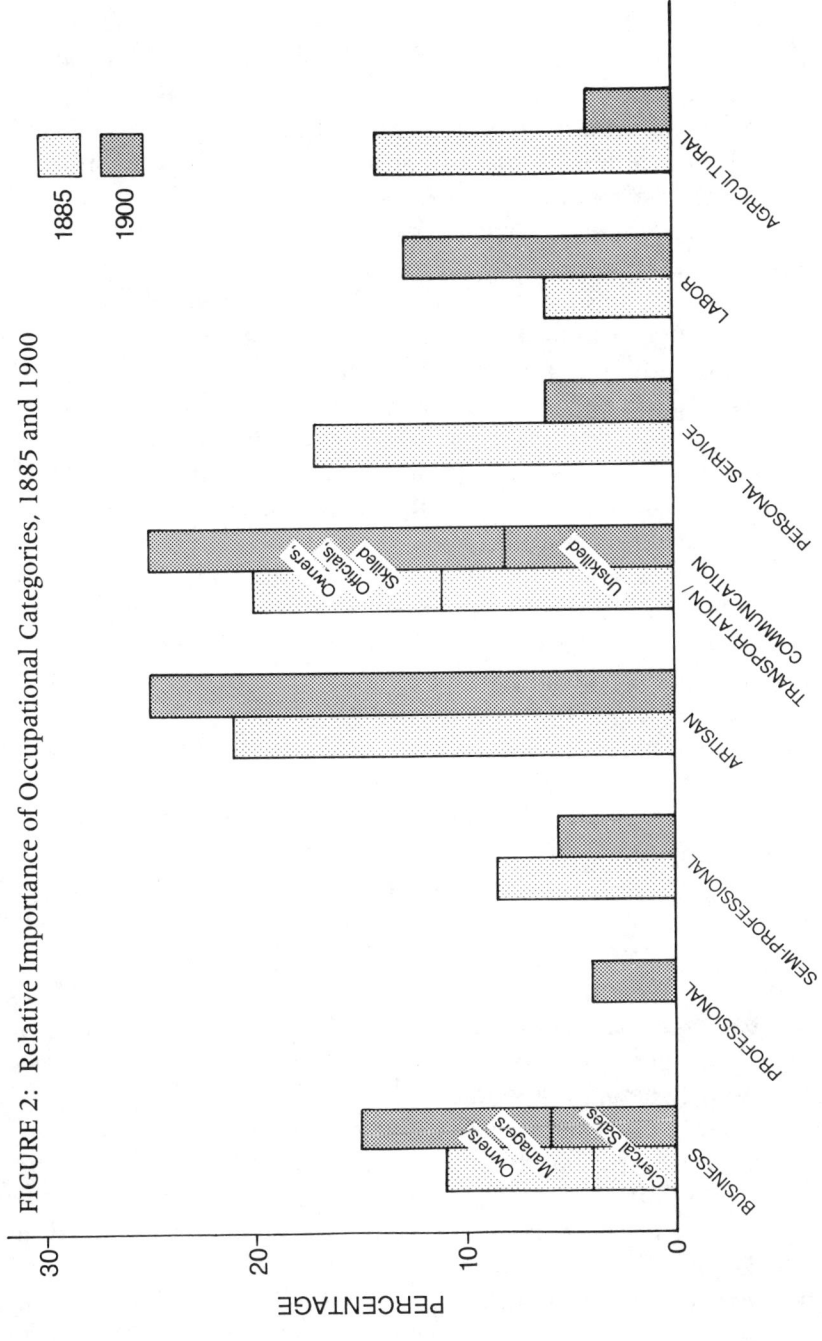

FIGURE 2: Relative Importance of Occupational Categories, 1885 and 1900

much of that well-being was due to the railroad. The location of a roundhouse in Grand Junction insured employment for those adept at railroad repair and maintenance. Because the town was also a divisional headquarters, engineers, conductors, and brakemen likewise took up residence. In 1900, almost a third of Grand Junction's skilled work force was on the railroad payroll.[27]

By 1900 a high degree of occupational specialization had emerged among the skilled trades in Grand Junction. Many of the jobs associated with the railroad, in particular, were specifically defined. In addition to such commonplace railroad occupations as those of conductors, brakemen, and engineers, there were car inspectors, coach cleaners, and carriage painters.[28] Other occupations also demonstrated specialization, although not to the extent of those involved with the railroad. In 1885, carpenters, painters, and bricklayers filled the ranks of the construction trade; by 1900 these workers had been joined by plasterers, glazers, and electricians

At first glance, it appears that the fraction of the work force providing personal services declined, especially in hotels, boarding and lodging houses, and restaurants. In 1885, the service sector made up 13.7 percent of Grand Junction's employment picture; in 1900, only 4.1 percent. But such an accounting examines only those people who actually named a job title when, in June 1900, census enumerator Nannie Forry asked, "Occupation?" It ignores the households that took in boarders and thereby furnished such "personal service." Now that Grand Junction was comprised mostly of families, there were proportionately fewer unmarried males in need of such services. Yet, because of population increase, the number of single males had increased, as had the number of single females.[29] Regardless of sex, however, most singles resided in family settings as boarders: one of eight households contained at least one boarder or lodger. As a result, hotels, and to a certain extent, restaurants and bakeries turned to travelers for customers.[30]

In addition to business activity and occupational diversification, the acquisition of property and wealth furnishes a third measure of economic opportunity in Grand Junction.[31] The price of town property was quite low—lots could be purchased for as little as ten dollars in 1885—and most who wanted to purchase could be expected to do so. At the same time, however, wealth, as measured by taxable assets, tended to be controlled by a smaller proportion of the population. The literature pertaining to wealth distribution on the frontier suggests that as population concentrated, so did wealth. The Grand Junction case conforms to these findings. County-level studies have demonstrated that the top 10 percent of the property holders controlled nearly 40 percent of the wealth. Towns exaggerated this concentration: there, the wealthiest decile controlled about half of the taxable property. In 1885, 44.7 percent of Grand Junction's taxable wealth was held by 10 percent of the property holders; fifteen years later, the top decile controlled half of the wealth.[32]

Despite this trend toward an increased concentration of wealth, the opportunity to own property did not diminish. Unlike towns settled for a longer time where access to property was limited because of lack of availability or high prices, Grand Junction remained a place where, from the outset, anyone who wanted to purchase property could do so. In the first few years, residential lots varied from ten dollars to one hundred dollars. By 1900, the cheapest residential property without improvements had increased to only thirty dollars, and in the additions made to the town, lots remained even less expensive. In Mobley's subdivision, for example, a lot cost half as much.[33] Yet cost did not seem to be the sole factor in the decision to invest, and much of Grand Junction's property remained unsold. Almost half of the property that did sell belonged to "absentee owners": people who paid taxes but were not listed in the local census. Of the 271 households taxed by Mesa County in 1885, for holding property in the town, some 122 (45.0 percent) were not counted in the census; in 1900, 685 households were taxed, while 336 (49.1 percent) were absentee landowners. Discovering just who these absentees were is almost impossible. Undoubtedly, some owners were residents of the town who were missed by the enumerator, but others did not live in the community.[34]

If property was so inexpensive, why did more than half the households refrain from landownership? Only 40 percent of the 1885 households purchased land, and that proportion declined to 30 percent in 1900. Part of the answer rests with the transient nature of the frontier and is attributable to research that relies on the census to measure resident populations. Given the "snapshot" nature of the U.S. Census, which counts people where they *are* rather than where they *live*, it is difficult to discern who truly constitutes the resident population intent on building a community. Thus, Grand Junction's 1885 census included such people as travelers and migrants passing through the community. (At the same time, it excluded residents who happened to be visiting or were away on business.) As will be discussed more fully in a later chapter, perhaps as many as one-third of those cataloged in 1885 by census enumerator W. A. Marsh had no intention of purchasing Grand Junction property because they planned to settle elsewhere. Though flawed, the census nevertheless provides such data as age, stage in the life cycle, and occupation—data that are valuable for describing households that acquired property.

The decision to purchase property depended on stages in the life cycle: married people were much more likely to own land than were single persons.[35] For the pioneer period, the stage in the life cycle is the only characteristic that helps in explaining property ownership, as Table 3 points out. Married households comprised 48.7 percent of the population, but they made up almost 60 percent of the property holders. Accordingly, single households comprised slightly more than one-half of the population, yet they accounted for only 40 percent of the property. Neither age nor occupation distinguished the households that decided to purchase property in the pioneer settlement. Although the youngest household heads were less likely to be owners, in general those with property reflected the population. Similarly, property owners were drawn from all occupational categories.[36]

Over time, married people continued to purchase property in larger proportions than single persons. In 1900, married households constituted 81.1 percent of the community, but they now comprised almost 90 percent of the property-owning group. Occupation also distinguished property owners. Heads of household who were in business or members of a profession were more likely to buy property than those in transportation and communication. The impermanence that often characterized the lives of people associated with the railroad undoubtedly contributed to their reluctance to purchase land.[37]

The inclination of those persons who purchased property to hold the same lots over a period of time provides additional evidence of the desire to build a new community. Regardless of when owners purchased land, so long as they remained in the town they retained the same lots. There were sixty-two property owners who persisted in Grand Junction from 1885 to 1900; of that number, all but two held their original lots. This tendency to own the same property over time suggests that the decision to purchase reflected a commitment

Table 3
Age, Life Cycle, and Occupation of Property Holders

	1885		1900	
	% in total population	% among prop. hold.	% in total population	% among prop. hold.
Percent households with property		40.7		31.2
A. Age				
18–29	31.4	26.0	14.3	4.6
30–39	39.1	43.5	31.0	28.5
40–49	17.1	15.3	30.8	35.9
50+	12.4	15.3	23.9	31.0
B. Life Cycle Stage				
Single	51.3	40.5	18.9	10.3
Never married	(40.4)	(34.4)	(13.3)	(7.5)
Ever married	(10.9)	(6.1)	(5.6)	(2.8)
Married	48.7	59.5	81.1	89.7
No children	(12.7)	(16.8)	(14.4)	(14.2)
Children	(32.9)	(38.9)	(60.7)	(71.2)
Single parent	(3.1)	(3.8)	(6.0)	(4.3)
C. Occupation				
Business	13.4	19.8	10.7	19.9
Professional	5.9	5.3	3.9	5.7
Semiprofessional	9.0	8.4	8.7	13.9
Artisan	25.2	27.5	20.0	20.6
Trans./Comm.	10.2	7.6	25.1	14.6
Personal Service	7.1	6.1	5.3	3.6
Agriculture	11.8	11.5	4.7	5.0
Labor	9.9	8.4	11.6	5.0
Other	7.5	5.3	10.1	11.7
N	322	131	980	281

to the community as well as the desire to own land. Lots were priced in a way that might encourage speculation (as already noted, a high proportion of the owners did not reside in Grand Junction), but among those who lived in the community, a domicile, rather than a gamble, was their principal concern. Those settlers who put their faith in Grand Junction and stayed to mature with the pioneer settlement bought town lots and built homes in which to raise their children. Charles and Nettie McCarey erected their home on White Avenue, between Second and Third streets, and never moved. Similarly, Harvey Bucklin bought lots two blocks away, on Grand Avenue, next to those of his brother James. Harvey and his wife Maggie still resided on that property in 1900. The Bucklins had stable neighbors as well. Adjacent to James's property was the home of his law partner, Lorin Staley, and across the street were William and Americas Lesher and their two children.

The economic processes that transformed Grand Junction from a pioneer settlement into a stable small town were reflected in the community's changed business environment and occupational structure. The multiplication of families also characterized community maturation and, at the same time, had an impact on the economic arena. Families were much more likely to purchase property in the community. In addition, the families that settled Grand Junction followed the nineteenth-century practice of taking in boarders and lodgers, and by 1900 few single people lived alone or in hotels or boardinghouses. Consequently, the occupational structure was affected: there was less demand for such personal service jobs as launderer or cook because these tasks were included in the boarding arrangement. Such alterations also encouraged a degree of intimacy—at least for the single people, who now resided in the more personal atmosphere of a family rather than in a hotel or boardinghouse.

The families that settled in Grand Junction influenced much more than the economic fabric. They faced a variety of issues as they created this new community: the funding of education and the control of liquor, prostitution, and gambling, for example. However, the most important problem in this arid territory west of the Rocky Mountains centered on obtaining water; and between 1882 and 1900, Grand Junction residents tried several solutions. The process was not without conflict, and as the next chapter points out, the dominance of the Grand Junction Town Company diminished as a result.

George A. Crawford, "Father of Grand Junction." Town builder and president of the Grand Junction Town Company. Museum of Western Colorado.

James W. Bucklin, Mayor, 1886–1887. Lawyer, politician, and leader in the drive for municipal ownership of water. Museum of Western Colorado.

Monroe L. Allison, Mayor, 1893–1897. Town promoter and activist against the Grand Junction Water Company. Colorado Historical Society.

Wendall P. Ela, Mayor, 1897–1901. Cattleman and banker; coalition mayor who united the town for municipal control and mountain water. Ela Family Private Collection.

The first log dwelling in the pioneer settlement, 1881. R. D. Mobley, left. Museum of Western Colorado.

Shortly after the school board was elected in 1882, pioneers built a schoolhouse and hired Nannie Blain to teach. Colorado Historical Society.

Powerhouse of the Grand Junction Water Company, about 1889. Museum of Western Colorado.

Office of the Grand Junction Town Company, 1882. Colorado Historical Society.

The demand that the "Utes Must Go" was so pervasive that it appeared even in newspaper ads. Colorado Historical Society.

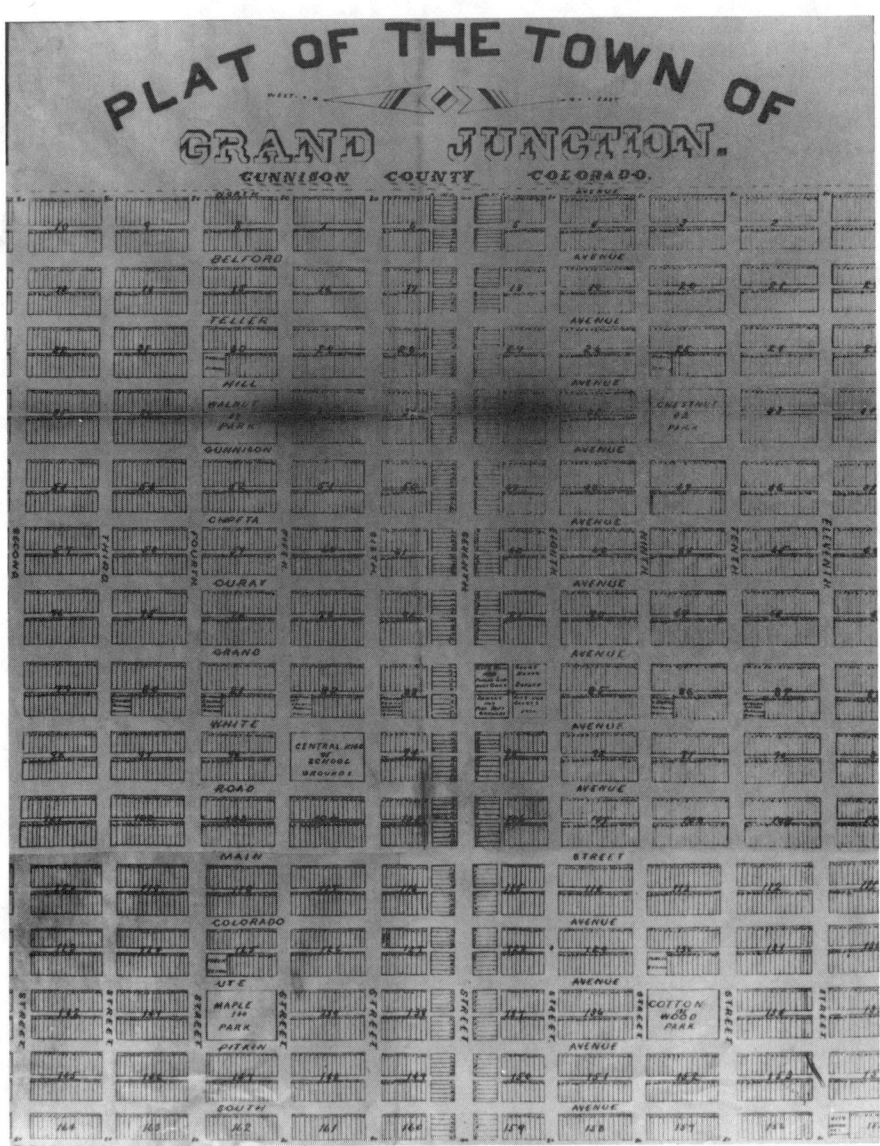

The original plat of Grand Junction, showing land set aside for schools, churches, and public buildings.

Looking southwest from Fifth and Main, 1884. Colorado Historical Society.

Same view, about fifteen years later. In front, right, is the Grand Valley National Bank; the domed building in the center is the Canon Building, which housed the Mesa County Bank. Museum of Western Colorado.

Main Street, 1884, looking east from Fourth Street. Denver Public Library, Western History Department.

Looking northeast from Fifth and Main, 1884. The area in the background would later become Grand Junction's residential section. Colorado Historical Society.

Same view, 1891, from the top of the Canon Building. Museum of Western Colorado.

Same view, about 1910. The tall building in the right center replaced the Grand Valley National Bank Building. The Denver Public Library, Western History Department.

View from the Grand Junction Water Company's standpipe at the corner of Seventh and Ouray, 1889. Museum of Western Colorado.

Company F, Grand Valley Guards, 1885. Colorado Historical Society.

Amazon Guards, auxiliary to Company F, 1890. Museum of Western Colorado.

Grand Junction Wheelmen, 1897. Museum of Western Colorado.

Ladies Columbine Band, 1900. Museum of Western Colorado.

3 · COMMUNITY DECISION MAKING

"Water ... at any price"[1]

In most new communities on the American frontier, the establishment of a governmental framework was among the highest priorities. Grand Junction was no exception.[2] By June 1882, enough people had arrived in Grand Junction to meet the state's population requirement for incorporating a settlement. In July, those settlers elected a mayor and four aldermen. Grand Junction again benefited from the town-building experience of pioneers like George A. Crawford. Under Crawford's direction, the Grand Junction Town Company carried out the initial work of platting the town. Company officers R. D. Mobley and James Bucklin were instrumental in organizing the meeting that requested town incorporation. In the late summer of 1882, when the first mayor filed for a patent on the newly incorporated townsite, the company paid the mayor's expenses to the federal land office in Leadville. The following year, Crawford and Monroe L. Allison, another official in the town company, helped to convince the state legislature to divide Colorado's western slope into several smaller counties and to name Grand Junction as seat of one of those counties.[3]

The initial willingness of new settlers to accommodate to the company's physical scheme and political maneuverings did not mean that they acceded to the firm in all matters. Although the company retained a financial interest in Grand Junction until 1899, within a few years of settlement the residents began to level criticism at company officers, whose influence then began to wane. Facilitating the challenges were the annual municipal and special elections, in which residents voiced their approval or disapproval of the community's political and institutional course.[4]

As in all new communities, the citizens of Grand Junction faced issues of social control—the control of vice and liquor, the provision of police and fire protection, the maintenance of streets and sidewalks—and sought ways in which to fund the solutions. In September 1882, the town's council met for the first time and began adopting rules to regulate the community. By 5 October, several "ordinances" were in effect, requiring licenses for many businesses; among them, "vendors of spirits and mault [sic] liquors," "hotel owners," "pawn brokers," and "intelligence brokers." Whether they simply enacted all the laws suggested by state guidelines or were anticipating problems, the aldermen also defined misdemeanors: impersonating an officer of the law; transvestism; cruelty to animals; drunkenness; and prostitution. Another set of misdemeanors dealt with public health and safety.[5]

Town ordinances prohibited, but could not completely eliminate, drunkenness and prostitution. Demands for Sunday closing and for temperance were sounded more frequently after 1893, when women in Colorado obtained the franchise, although these demands always met with opposition from saloon owners and their patrons. Some Grand Junction residents actively supported the Prohibition party, and several stood as candidates for local and state office on that ticket. However, support for prohibition was not as widespread as it was vocal. In general elections between 1888 (when the Prohibition party was organized in Colorado) and 1900, the party in Mesa County and Grand Junction never garnered as much as 10 percent of the vote.[6]

Water, always a consideration in the arid West, became an even more hotly debated issue than prohibition.[7] From the outset, water aroused great concern among Grand Junction's residents, dominated aldermen's meetings, and eventually became the subject of a dozen special elections. Without water, no community could survive, and as historian James Edward Wright points out, "although [aridity] was a given topographical and climatological feature of the state, . . . propaganda of the early 1880s had assured potential settlers there was adequate water in Colorado."[8] The conflict over water, however, reveals more than the community's desire to attract settlers. It also shows that Grand Junction, though still very much a frontier town, was not isolated from the climate of municipal reform taking shape in the last quarter of the nineteenth century. Residents were anxious about public safety and health, and they wanted fire protection and quality domestic water. A few, among them attorney James W. Bucklin and George Smith (owner of a coal mine), focused on issues beyond the immediacy of obtaining water. As followers of Henry George and advocates of the Single Tax, these two men voiced concern about "control of monopolies" and "municipal ownership" very early in the discussion concerning water.[9]

Dissatisfaction first with the town company and then with an outside corporation evolved into a determination on the part of residents to control the water system themselves. The drive for municipal ownership was carried out over a thirteen-year period with frequent elections, intense infighting among townspeople, and a number of court cases. These developments acted as a catalyst in Grand Junction's political maturation, a maturation marked primarily by three phases. From the town's initial settlement to mid-1888, pioneers let the Grand Junction Town Company provide water, although by 1886 they began to seek alternatives. From July 1888 until December 1894, residents permitted a company owned principally by outsiders to furnish water, but only under a franchise that they believed would protect them. This marked a major step in the community's evolution from pioneer settlement to small town. When residents voted in December 1894 to build and operate a municipally owned water system, they embarked on a third stage of political maturation that carried with it greater public control of the community and an unshakeable confidence in Grand Junction's future.[10]

Doubtlessly, their preoccupation with such pressing necessities as erecting cabins and starting businesses prompted the settlers to rely at first on the Grand Junction Town Company's Pacific Slope Ditch for water. By 1886, however, they were vigorously challenging that reliance and searching for alternatives. They were especially angry at the company's water rates, which seemed excessive, and at its failure to provide any fire protection. "For the three years preceding," declared Edwin Price (now a town alderman) in the *Grand Junction News*, the community

> has paid $2,500 for irrigation alone. She has paid an equal amount to vendors of water on the streets and has had no protection against fire whatever. This is a large sum in the aggregate and it is time to do something.[11]

Other settlers echoed Price's sentiments, and in early April 1886, they looked to the town council to find another means for obtaining water. The council, headed by James Bucklin, named a committee "to solicit propositions for furnishing water to the town." Three weeks later, Martin Florida offered to provide water for two years. The minutes of the meeting fail to note the fee sought by Florida, but the council directed its water committee "to wait on George A. Crawford and offer him $300./yr for [a] three year term."[12] Crawford refused. A month later, as warm weather came to the Grand Valley, the council contracted with the Pacific Slope Ditch for a season's water at four hundred dollars. At the same time, however, the council explored the possibility of a permanent water supply. The council had the power to create an indebtedness to provide public services, but it decided to submit to the taxpayers "an issue of bonds for $10,000.00 to secure permanent water for the town."[13] Turnout at the 1 June 1886 election was "light," according to the newspaper report, but the response was affirmative.[14] Next, the council faced the problem of deciding the source of the town's water.

Artesian wells were one possibility. As early as 1883 some citizens had organized a company to sink wells and to solicit funds from the town's residents. Although the scheme proved unsuccessful, over the next several years artesian wells remained a much-discussed possibility for a source of water. Another possible source was the Denver and Rio Grande Railway's pump on the Gunnison River. Some town council members believed that the railroad might agree to meet Grand Junction's water needs. That possibility ended in the summer of 1886, when the Denver and Rio Grande became preoccupied with its own problems of foreclosure and reorganization.[15]

A third option involved a system of reservoirs located to trap water from the Gunnison. This plan, which was the first to provoke much interest, called for granting a franchise to a private company represented by Thomas C. Clayton, businessman and attorney, to provide fire hydrants at strategic locations and domestic water at an annual rate of two thousand dollars. Clayton's plan caught the council's attention, but by law any decision pertaining to franchises required voter approval. The town council accordingly set an election for 2 November 1886. Clayton called a public meeting prior to the election so that he might explain his plans and rate schedules. The desire for such information was keen, and according to the *News*, the "house was filled by representative citizens and those who were interested."[16]

Two issues dominated the public discussions: cost and ownership. George Crawford questioned whether the town could afford a water system of such magnitude, and gave his views about the "practicability of the city undertaking the matter." George Smith, publicly the first to advocate municipal ownership, argued that community control of the utility was preferable to the establishment of a private syndicate; indeed, Smith saw little difference between the present company and the proposed franchise plans. He said he found himself "standing between two monopolies." Mayor James Bucklin ended the meeting with a "ringing speech." He "believed the time had come when a water system was necessary . . . for the sake of humanity, of life and of health, as a means of advertisement and to meet the crying need of the hour."[17] However, arguments against the franchise apparently were more persuasive because voters defeated the plan. The council subsequently negotiated with the town company to provide water for 1887.

The search for alternatives continued. Residents demanded what they termed a "permanent" water supply, which provided for fire protection and domestic water usage. Late in the summer of 1887, Walter S. Binning petitioned the council for a special election to authorize the erection of a "Holly Water Works"—a system that relied on wells sunk near the Gunnison River. The council complied and set an election for early September. Thomas C. Clayton asked that his reservoir scheme be reconsidered at the same time, and the council reworded the election resolution to authorize the building of a "suitable water works." Unsure of the long-term viability of either plan, the council postponed the election and named aldermen J. W. Bridges, S. J. Scoville, and H. H. Rea to investigate ways that other Colorado towns obtained their water, especially those with municipally owned systems. For the first time, the council addressed the possibility of mountain water and also asked the committee to explore Whitewater Mesa, a low plateau about fifteen miles southeast of the town, as a possible source.

The committee reported in favor of the "Whitewater Plan," which called for a pipeline from the head of Whitewater Creek, a flume across the mesa, and a reservoir to hold the water for municipal use. It estimated a cost of eighty thousand dollars. The council approved the Whitewater Plan, and called an election to determine if voters shared their enthusiasm. Clayton and Binning, proponents of the other plans, voiced their opposition. The majority of the taxpayers agreed with the opposition and rejected the Whitewater Plan.[18]

December 1887 found the council once again trying to negotiate with the Denver and Rio Grande about the possibility of sharing its facilities. At approximately the same time, the council discussed Kansas businessman N. J. Krusen's offer to build a water system that would provide for fire protection, domestic use, and irrigation in exchange for a long-term franchise. Krusen asked for 3,750 dollars per year to provide water from the Gunnison River for fire protection and for use in public buildings. Residential water would cost nine dollars each year and irrigation twenty dollars annually. He promised to begin work on the water system as soon as the town agreed to his proposal. Over the next several months, aldermen and townspeople discussed Krusen's proposal as well as municipal ownership. "The water question is now the most important issue before the people," reported Edwin Price in the *News*. "Public opinion is somewhat divided as to whether we shall let a company have a franchise and put in a system or whether the town should construct and run its own works."[19]

On 1 May, the voters of Grand Junction confronted for the first time the issue of whether they wanted the responsibility of building and operating their own water system or were willing to grant a franchise. In a *News* editorial, Edwin Price voiced the concerns of those who believed in municipal ownership: "the city can put in and operate the water system as cheaply as a company, and also derive a revenue with which we can pay the principal and interest on the cost of same." Still, the editorial continued, "the voting of a franchise for twenty-one years is a serious matter, and means that the people shall be subject to whatever treatment a company may see fit to give them." Price's admonition went unheeded as voters approved the concession to Krusen.[20]

Less than a month passed before the council received a petition from fifty-three businessmen "asking for a special election to consider the Krusen water works." Petitioners were concerned with the location of the pumping plant and the standpipe, which would be located outside the town limits. Instead, they proposed that water from the Grand River be used so that "the whole system [would be] within the corporate limits of the town, and therefore liable to taxation, a very considerable advantage to the town." The businessmen also raised questions about the terms of hydrant rental. The council honored the request and scheduled an election for 3 July 1888.[21]

The second election permitted those opposed to the franchise another chance to defeat the plan. George Crawford, president of the Grand Junction Town Company and the Pacific Slope Ditch, called a public meeting just before the election, and according to the *News*, "all the speeches that were made reflected upon the integrity and sincerity of the Krusen company."[22] Turnout at the public meeting was large, but Crawford and others who opposed the franchise failed to persuade the voters. The franchise was again approved, this time by a three-to-one margin.[23]

Crawford's unsuccessful attempt to defeat the Krusen franchise reflected his own waning popularity as well as that of the town company. An especially outspoken critic was Edwin Price, editor of the *Grand Junction News*. Price and his printing press had been brought to Grand Junction at the town company's expense in 1882, and at first Price had nothing but praise for Crawford and the company. In 1883, when an "anti–town company movement" emerged in Grand Junction, Price defended the company and Crawford.[24] Initial discord between Price and the town company may have stemmed from political differences—the *News* remained loyal to the Republican party, while many of the men associated with the Grand Junction Town Company were first Democrats and later Populists. Regardless of whether politics played a role, by 1887 the *News* was openly critical of the town company. Price was particularly incensed at the company's failure to promote Grand Junction and its lack of "confidence in the location of the town and its future." "The company seems to be making no effort to get new enterprises established," Price declared in May 1888. "This may suit Governor Crawford and his friends, but it does not suit the people who live here."[25]

Also contributing to dissatisfaction with the company were decisions from the department of the interior that negated the town's patent and thereby questioned the titles held by individuals to town lots. These were decisions upholding the claims of William Keith to a portion of Section 14. Ten days after Crawford, Mobley, and Warner had staked their claim in September 1881, William Keith took up a preemption claim that included a portion of that section. Following preemption rules, Keith remained in residence and built a cabin. In January 1882, when the Grand Junction Town Company began a formal survey, Keith tried to prevent the inclusion of his claim and twice removed the surveyor's markings. The town company filed a civil complaint, and Keith was arrested on 3 January 1882. A week later, he was found guilty, and the town company proceeded with its survey. When residents incorporated Grand Junction on 22 June 1882, no one was residing on the disputed property. Keith did not give up, however. On 26 September 1882, Keith once more filed his claim, and on 1 December of that year, he tried to complete his proof. Challenged again by the town company, Keith sued. The resultant hearing found in favor of the town (on 4 October 1883) and Keith appealed. Ultimately, the case was reviewed by the secretary of the interior, Henry M. Teller, who reversed the previous decision and canceled the town's entry on Keith's claim.[26] Teller concluded that while both Keith and the Grand Junction Town Company had filed on the land prematurely, Keith was a bona fide settler and the town company officers were not. The town and the town company appealed twice, but the secretary's decision remained firm.

Keith's suit also brought into question the titles held by individuals to town lots as well as the town's own property. When Keith's claim was declared valid in 1888, the town company came under attack. "Keith was the victim," the *News* heralded, "of a dirty conspiracy here in the early days; he was treated shamefully by the Town Company and its hangers-on."[27] While the newspaper condemned the town company, the aldermen filed lawsuits for fraud against both Crawford and the company. A citizen's committee, created by the Board of Trade and comprised of a dozen businessmen commissioned to inquire into "the causes of the present stagnation in all kinds of businesses" as well as "the apparent cloud of title to realty in our city," submitted a resolution to the aldermen asking that they drop the litigation. "The public interests," declared the resolution, "would be subserved by the dismissal of such suits." The *News* retorted that the citizen's committee had been "in reality appointed by one man"—Crawford. The signatures of 120 residents belied the *News*'s assertion, and the lawsuits were dropped.[28] About six months later, and after a federal land office investigation, the town received its patent and residents secured titles to their land. Nevertheless, the impact of Keith's lawsuit and the ensuing charges of fraud leveled at the town company was long lasting. Although some individuals associated with the company, like M. L. Allison, who later served as mayor, remained active in Grand Junction politics, the company itself retreated from the political scene.

Voters in Grand Junction had now twice approved Krusen's request for a water franchise. By so doing, they had refused to risk municipal ownership, but by rejecting the wishes of Crawford and the town company they had taken a fledgling step toward independence. After six years of inadequate fire protection and of being subjected to a variety of proposed solutions, residents now looked forward to an improved water system. According to the terms of the franchise approved in July 1888, the Krusen Company received a twenty-one-year charter. In exchange, the company promised to provide water "of good quality and fit for domestic use" at the cost of a dollar a month to single-family residences. The provisions for fire protection were quite specific: fire hydrants had to be "capable of discharging four one-inch streams from any four hydrants through fifty feet of two and one-half inch rubber hose and one inch nozzle to a height of seventy-five feet in any part of the town." Annual rental for fifty hydrants was set at 3,750 dollars.[29]

Their expectations were short lived. Over the next several months, the council and the water company ironed out the details of the franchise contract, with hydrant rental taking up much of the attention. Though the residents approved the 3,750-dollar figure, town attorney Lorin A. Staley drew attention to Colorado statutes limiting the rate of taxation that could be levied to provide water. In Grand Junction, the rental fee sought by the water company was triple the amount allowed under state law.[30] At first, the council balked at the fee, but after four months of discussion, the council majority decided to ignore the statute. At the same time, however, it also bargained for a reduction in the hydrant rental fee. Finally, in late November 1888, the council and the Grand Junction Water Company compromised: hydrant rental would be 3,250 dollars, and the contract was signed.[31] By the end of the year construction was under way, with the promise that the plant would be functioning by April 1889; in fact, the water system was not in service until August, but that was within the limitations stipulated by the contract.

In February 1889, scarcely a month after the contract was signed, the Grand Junction Water Company became the focus of concern when Thomas H. Hadcock accused his fellow aldermen—S. J. Scoville, David Roberts, H. H. Rea, and J. J. Lumsden—of lobbying for the water company's franchise in exchange for building contracts.

Hadcock charged that Lumsden had promised him all the smithing work (as well as a cash bonus) if he voted with the majority of the council in favor of the water company's contract. Hadcock later revealed the offer to another alderman, John Hynes. Hynes advised Hadcock "to keep quiet and let things take their course." Subsequently, Hadcock alleged that he had again been offered a bribe, this time for his support of the council's decision to ignore the state restrictions and for his approval of the rental-fee compromise. Hadcock once more turned to Hynes for counsel. Hynes said that Hadcock "ought to expose them." Hadcock "soon afterwards told several persons I had been approached and offered money for my vote." His remarks caught the attention of the *Mesa County Democrat*, a newspaper linked to George A. Crawford.[32]

At the public hearing requested by Hadcock, others corroborated the charges. George Currie, a contractor, testified that the street gossip centered on a conspiracy among the aldermen, but he denied having any firsthand information. A more direct accusation came from Joseph A. Hunt, who said that even though his bid to construct the water company's building had been lower than Lumsden's the contract had gone to Lumsden. In defense, the water company's engineer, J. S. Simmons, maintained that in every case he took the lowest bid. Moreover, each of the aldermen denied any involvement with bribery. A citizen's committee, appointed by the mayor to investigate the accusations, uncovered no evidence that bribes had been offered or received. On the other hand, the committee studiously refused to make any judgment about the truth of the accusations. The bribery hearing delayed construction for only a few days, but the allegations eroded community support for the Krusen company.[33]

No sooner had the bribery controversy subsided than another problem emerged. Complaints about the quality of materials stalled the work and caused some residents to ask the council "to prevent the Water Company from putting in the pipe scattered through the streets." A company representative responded with what must have been convincing evidence of the pipe's quality because the complaint was shelved for the time.[34] In late June 1889, the pumping station passed its first test by exhibiting adequate pressure for domestic use. Six weeks later, the station demonstrated that it had the necessary water pressure in the hydrants. Satisfied with the experiments, the council passed an ordinance stating that the water company had carried out its part of the contract.[35]

For the next nine or ten months, relations between the council and the water company were amiable, and focused on extending the water works to new areas. However, the spring thaw of 1890 was heavy, causing the level of the Grand River to rise dangerously and to carry a great deal of sediment downstream. When sediment began to appear in house taps throughout Grand Junction, citizens accused the water company of not complying with that portion of the contract requiring adequate filtering processes. The failure of the company to provide water of "good quality" prompted the aldermen to refuse payment of the annual rental fee in October 1890.

The following February, the water company once more presented its bills and again the council refused to pay, arguing that the poor water quality was evidence that the company had defaulted on the contract. Winter runoff in 1891 again forced sediment into the town's water supply, and discontent about inadequate filtering held the council's attention throughout most of that season. The water company was not unresponsive to these complaints, and installed additional filtering reservoirs; nevertheless, in late summer the council reaffirmed its earlier decision and spurned demands for hydrant rents.[36]

By September 1891, when the council again refused to pay its rental, three camps had developed in Grand Junction on the issue of water. The first consisted of persons who supported the Grand Junction Water Company. They believed that the franchise represented the best solution to the water problem, and insisted that the town honor its contract with the water company. The other two camps were hostile to the water company. In one were long-time advocates of municipal ownership, like James Bucklin and George Smith, and in the other were people, like M. L. Allison, who were simply opposed to this particular company rather than advocates of public control. Allison led the fight against the water company, first as an alderman and then for four years as mayor. He later became a strong supporter of mountain water. Most Grand Junction residents were in none of the camps, but by the end of the decade there was widespread public sentiment demanding that the water problem be resolved.[37]

Frustration with the water situation prompted the council to annul the franchise in April 1892, and over the next two years to seek alternative sources of water. Proponents of mountain water convinced the council to investigate nearby springs and streams. A committee reported that springs on Piñon Mesa, about twenty miles southwest of the town, could be developed for three hundred dollars.[38] A few months later, advocates of artesian water put forth a plan, as they had several years earlier, and at a special election held in November 1893, voters approved a twenty-year franchise for the Western Colorado Development Company to dig wells.[39]

Neither mountain water nor artesian wells solved Grand Junction's immediate water problem. No action was taken on the Piñon Mesa proposal, and the promoters of artesian wells faced several delays.[40] Public concern intensified, and in May 1894, W. S. Sullivan, an attorney and pioneer settler, presented to the aldermen a citizen's petition seeking a special election to approve fifty thousand dollars for the purchase of the existing water system. Encouraged by the citizen's request, the council dispatched a committee to "ascertain what [the water company] will take for the water works system as it is."[41] Uninterested in selling, the company seemed willing to repair the system if the council would pay the back rent due on hydrants. At first the council agreed, but before a resolution written to address the compromise could be approved, the public mounted a campaign against it.

"A large crowd . . . assembled" at the aldermen's October meeting and presented a "lengthy petition . . . which contained a long list of signatures," objecting to the inefficiency of the existing works and demanding an election on the issue of bringing in mountain water. Not everyone agreed. Alderman J. L. Pratt argued that such an election would be unfair because it would "act as a lever to beat down the true value of [the water company's] plant." The debate persuaded the council to abrogate its agreement with the water company. Instead, aldermen named Mayor M. L. Allison and two other councilmen as a committee to

> ascertain the price demanded for the old plant, . . . the probable amount of bonds necessary to build a new system, [and to] find the water supply and report to the next meeting of the council[,] and if the report be favorable to immediately call an election.[42]

The investigative committee submitted a report at the November meeting that advocated the streams of Grand Mesa, a high plateau about 30 miles east of Grand Junction, as the best source of water. A. J. McCune, a consultant to the committee, outlined how the water could be routed through the mountains to the town. Acting on the advice of the engineer of the Denver Water Company, Mayor Allison estimated that water could be provided to 30,000 people at a cost of 225,000 dollars. (Grand Junction's population at this time was about 2,700.) The council was favorably disposed to the committee's findings, and set an election for 28 December 1894 to authorize the sale of bonds to fund this project.[43]

When the council advocated a public indebtedness amounting to almost a quarter of a million dollars, the general populace became more vocal. At the council meeting the following week, many townspeople objected to the size of the indebtedness and expressed fears that such an outlay would preclude any expenditures on such needed municipal improvements as sewers. Others raised questions about the bonds. Would they be discounted—that is, sold at less than face value—thereby obligating the town to pay interest on less capital than it actually received? Would the revenue generated from water patrons permit the town to meet the 5 percent interest payments to bondholders, an amount totalling 11,250 dollars annually? One person who voiced the latter concern was W. P. Dickenson, a stockholder in the Grand Junction Water Company. Dickenson reported that the annual receipts to that company were never more than eight thousand dollars. A. R. Wadsworth, a proponent of the bond scheme, disagreed. Wadsworth claimed that he had conducted an informal count of the number of homes connected to the water company lines, and he concluded that the water company revenues were more than double the amount claimed by Dickenson.[44]

Still another area of concern involved the quality and quantity of the proposed streams. Unpersuaded by the townspeople's objections, the council finalized the resolution for voter consideration. That resolution authorized a municipally owned water system that would be supplied by the streams of Grand Mesa. It created a bonded indebtedness of 250,000 dollars, with bonds being sold at par and paying 5 percent interest. Proceeds from customers of the water system would pay the interest; additional funds, if necessary, would be generated through taxation.[45]

During the weeks preceding the December election, a great deal of dialogue took place both in newspapers and at public meetings. Those favoring the ordinance dominated a public meeting called by Mayor M. L. Allison and chaired by James Bucklin. They denounced the "evils of cities giving away franchises," and underscored the need for water of better quality. In melding these two long-discussed issues, proponents were better able to garner support.[46] Opponents responded by scheduling a meeting of their own, where they reiterated their fears about the proposed indebtedness. John O'Boyle, a resident of twelve years, hinted at conspiracy. The men pushing the mountain-water scheme, argued O'Boyle, were speculators and wanted to create a boom, but "it was the poor man, with a little home, who expected to live here and die here that had to pay that great debt."[47] O'Boyle's indictment lacked evidence. Except for a few men in real estate, nothing suggests that the advocates of the resolution were speculators who would benefit from a boom. Although many of the strongest proponents of either mountain water or municipal ownership did have extensive property, so did several of those among the opposition. O'Boyle's defense of the "poor man" was also questionable. Though O'Boyle, a locomotive engineer, owned no real estate in 1894, he was taxed on 1,376 dollars in personal property—an amount roughly three times greater than the median assessment.[48]

The election resulted in a victory for mountain water. An estimated 88 percent of the eligible voters turned out, and three-fifths favored the ballot measure.[49] More importantly, citizens endorsed the concept of municipal ownership. Never again would they consider any plan for water that lacked local control. Still, the issue was far from resolved. The central question was whether the town should purchase the existing plant or build its own. Between this election in December 1894 and March 1900, when the municipal system was satisfactorily tested, the council found itself involved in constant litigation; the bonds did not sell; and attempts to purchase the Grand Junction Water Company were unsuccessful. The failure to resolve the water problem resulted first in a proliferation of single-issue political parties and then in the emergence of coalition parties, which incorporated "Citizen," "Home," or "Improvement" in their names. As a result, the community grew unified not only in support of municipal ownership, but also in a desire to build a wholly new system.

The later unity did not come easily. In January 1895, about a month after the election, the Grand Junction Water Company filed suit against the town council to recover 14,200 dollars for hydrant rentals. That April, the water company also sought an injunction to restrain the town from issuing and selling bonds that would underwrite the mountain-water plan. The dispute over hydrant rental went to trial the following spring. The town argued that the Grand Junction Water Company had not complied with its contract, and drew special attention to the poor-quality pipes and the presence of sediment in the domestic water. In rebuttal, water company officials claimed that they had provided adequate fire protection and had furnished "the best possible water supply within their power from the Grand river."[50] These arguments failed to impress the local jury, which found in favor of the town.

The water company appealed the case, and in February 1900, the Colorado Court of Appeals reversed the earlier decision on the grounds that the water company had fulfilled its contractual obligations. So far as the pipes were concerned, the court ruled that when councilmen certified the water company's completion of its contract in September 1889, they had approved the pipes.[51] Moreover, declared the court, the townspeople had also authorized the Grand River as the source of water, and the Grand Junction Water Company could not be held responsible for the river's impurities. This ruling, while resulting in back hydrant rents for the company, failed to sidetrack the town's attempt to obtain a water system of its own.[52]

The various injunctions filed by the water company proved troublesome, however. Constant litigation slowed the sale of bonds. Aldermen issued 200,000 dollars in bonds during the summer of 1894, and in October they accepted a discounted bid of 197,300 dollars from Colorado Fuel and Iron to market the bonds, with the proviso that if Colorado Fuel and Iron could not sell the bonds by the following June, the contract would be canceled.[53]

The bonds did not sell, and by summer 1896 the council again discussed the purchase of the Grand Junction Water Company. In September, the company initiated the first of three unsuccessful attempts to negotiate such an agreement by offering to turn over its system for 100,000 dollars. The aldermen believed the price was exorbitant—"far in excess of the value of the plant"—and concluded that "it seems useless to further consider this matter."[54] Three months later, however, the council offered the company 35,000 dollars for its works. While the water company considered the price too low, it countered with two suggestions: either the town buy the water company at a price determined by an independent committee, or the town could condemn the water company's property and take it over at a price set by the courts.

The council found neither of the propositions acceptable. Agreeing to either one, it believed, would be an "admission on the part of the city . . . that the . . . company had fully complied with the contract." In addition, arbitration

> would be an acknowledgement . . . the . . . company was entitled . . . to $3500 annually for [future] hydrant rentals . . . [and] an admission that the city owes said company the hydrant rental now sought to be adjusted in the courts amounting in round numbers to $18,000.[55]

At the March 1897 council meeting, the water company asked that voters be allowed to decide the question of purchase and that a ceiling price of 75,000 dollars be included on the ballot. When the council met to discuss the request, a large group of citizens attended and publicly debated the issue. One of them, Alvin Bucklin, who, like his brother James, advocated municipal ownership, introduced a counterproposal of his own. The so-called Bucklin Ordinance would authorize a 65,000-dollar indebtedness: 35,000 dollars to purchase the company's plant, and the remainder to repair the system. If the company refused the offer, then the entire sum would be applied to building a municipal system. The council agreed to put both his proposal and that of the company on the ballot for the regular election in April.[56]

In the three weeks between this action and the April election, advocates of each scheme campaigned arduously, and local newspapers mirrored those developments. The *Grand Junction News*, which still believed that the town had to honor its contract with the water company, charged that the "fight has become a personal one between the mayor and the water company—the one for control of the city and the other its life." The *News* assailed the Bucklin Ordinance as a "scheme . . . hatched in Denver by the mayor . . . for the purpose of counteracting any attempt to secure a settlement of the [water] trouble."[57] The *Grand Valley Star*, a proponent of municipal ownership, agreed that the controversy had now become a "plain showdown," but suggested that there was "no mystery or concealment about [Bucklin's plan]." "It presents a fair and square proposition to the people."[58]

The appearance of several political tickets testified to the friction in the town. In addition to the Republican and Populist tickets, two factions designated candidates for council vacancies. The "Bucklin Ordinance" campaigned for municipal ownership. The "Citizens and Taxpayers" took no open stance on water, but claimed to be "mainly interested in economy in city affairs." Prohibitionists also nominated candidates on the "No License League" ticket. The election was complicated because only those with real or personal property—whose taxes would pay interest on the bonds—could vote on the question of indebtedness, while all residents could select the mayor and council members. Each of the town's four wards had two representatives, elected for two-year terms. To ensure continuity on the council, aldermen faced elections in alternate years. Thus, in any spring campaign, four seats, one from each ward, were vacant. The mayor, chosen at large, also served two years.[59]

In the 1897 campaign, two wards elected aldermen committed to the Bucklin Ordinance; two named representatives loyal to major parties; and a coalition candidate, Wendell P. Ela, won the mayoral seat. Ela had run on three tickets: Citizens and Taxpayers, Populist, and Republican. About 360 property holders endorsed the Bucklin Ordinance by a two-to-one margin.[60] Following the course prescribed by the voters, the aldermen sought to exchange municipal bonds (valued at 35,000 dollars) for deeds to the Grand Junction Water Company's properties. The water company refused to accept the bonds because the proffered price was too low, but even if the dollar amount had been acceptable the company would probably have balked because of its fears about the strengths of the bonds.[61]

Negotiations between the council and the water company stalled. Then, in January 1898, residents, anxious that the water issue be settled, requested the council to raise the offer—from the 35,000 dollars authorized in the Bucklin Ordinance to 50,000 dollars. In the following month, the water company countered with a request for 60,000 dollars. Aldermen answered with 55,000 dollars, which the water company accepted, causing the *News* prematurely to headline "City Ownership in Sight."[62]

Alderman A. T. Wharton, a supporter of mountain water, asked the council to submit the purchase agreement to the voters, but the council refused. Most aldermen wanted to avoid having their success undone at the ballot box, since the arrangement with the water company assured a higher price than taxpayers had authorized. They had the support, moreover, of many citizens, and several who were present at the council meeting spoke in favor of the agreement. One, Dr. Heman Bull, declared that purchasing the water company would end "the bitter warfare that had been going on to the town's detriment for so many years." A half-dozen business and professional men seconded Bull's endorsement. Not easily put off, M. L. Allison and others among the opposition filed an injunction to prevent the council from finalizing the purchase without an election. Rather than wait several months for a court decision on the injunction, the council placed the purchase agreement on the April ballot.[63]

As in the preceding year, there were two elections: one to elect four aldermen, and the other to decide the purchase agreement. Several factions were again represented: "Citizens and Taxpayers," "Citizens League," and "Home Protection." Concern over the water issue was evident in the voter turnout. Slightly more than half of the 1,900 eligible voters cast ballots to elect the council, but almost nine-tenths of the approximate 370 taxpayers voted. They approved the purchase agreement by a five-to-three margin.[64]

The summer of 1898 must have reminded aldermen of the previous summer as they tried to get the deeds to the water company's property. For reasons that are unclear, company attorney Charles Caswell did not deliver any documents until early autumn. By then most council members believed that the water company was "still using dilatory tactics," and they recommended "no further negotiations." The board's minority sought to keep the bargaining possibilities open, and when a resolution addressing the futility of continued talks was introduced, the minority members—Starr, McKinney, and Hadcock—walked out and left the council without a quorum. The split between the minority, which favored purchase, and the majority, which opposed it, persisted for the next two years.[65]

The council majority reflected a shift in public sentiment. By the end of 1898, residents were tired of what they viewed as insouciance on the part of the Grand Junction Water Company, and favored the erection of a separate plant. When Caswell finally produced the water company deeds and demanded that they be exchanged for municipal bonds, it was too late. The council rescinded its previous offer, and looked instead toward a new system. The water company made a final attempt to sell at a reduced price of 49,000 dollars in the summer of 1899. The election that September underscored the community's determination. An estimated 86 percent of the eligible voters turned out to reject the offer, with slightly over 60 percent voting no.[66]

By late spring 1899, the council's full attention was on building the town's own water plant. Aldermen named an agent to market the 65,000 dollars in bonds voted two years earlier, and within weeks, a Colorado Springs bank had accepted the bonds. At about the same time, a Denver engineer presented plans and speculated that the Grand Junction Water Company's holdings could be duplicated for as little as 25,000 dollars. (In fact, the town would incur 87,000 dollars in debts to fund the system.) In June, the council approved the blueprints and advertised for bids in engineering magazines.[67] In early autumn, it named a contractor and construction began. Building proceeded rapidly, and in February 1900 the town successfully conducted a preliminary test of its water system. In April, the entire town drew water from the municipal plant.[68]

Completion of the waterworks did not heal the wounds of a decade of controversy. Grand Junction was far from united, as the indictment and conviction for bribery of aldermen Reuben Starr and Andrew McKinney in October 1899 pointed out. They were accused of offering five hundred dollars to alderman A. T. Wharton to vote for the purchase of the Grand Junction Water Company. Arguing that they could not get a fair trial in Grand Junction and claiming that they had been threatened, the defendants asked for a change of venue. Their request was denied, and shortly thereafter, the two were convicted. Within a week of sentencing, the Colorado Supreme Court stayed the judgment, pending a review. A year later, in December 1900, the higher court overturned the conviction because of procedural errors.[69]

The conviction and stay of sentencing raised issues demonstrating that the council was still divided over municipal ownership and mountain water. As soon as Starr and McKinney were sentenced, four members of the council—all advocates of mountain water—voted for replacements. The remainder of the council—Mayor Ela and two aldermen—refused to participate in the election or to attend subsequent meetings. City attorney J. S. Carnahan admonished the council that the "men elected . . . had no legal rights as councilmen," and the clerk, M. O. Delaplain, withheld the oath of office. Nevertheless, the substitutes, Charles P. McCary and Henry Kippe, were sworn in, and for a week the council functioned without the mayor, two aldermen, the clerk, and the attorney.[70] When the state supreme court issued a writ pointing out errors in the conduct of the case in the lower court and agreed to hear the case, Starr and McKinney reclaimed their seats. The *Daily Sentinel* reported, however, that the conviction of Starr and McKinney so tainted the two that councilmen Wharton, J. H. Ramey, and John Dickerson "found themselves being contaminated by sitting as members of the Aldermanic body," and they refused to "sit with the balance of the council."[71]

Within a month all regularly elected members were in attendance, but the water issue remained volatile. Although the new municipal system was almost complete, the years of discord had left a legacy of deep partisanship. Two years later, district attorney Samuel G. McMullin summarized that partisanship in a brief explaining why he would not prosecute Starr and McKinney further. The charges, McMullin pointed out,

> arose during a contest between citizens and interests in the City of Grand Junction concerning the erection and construction of a city water works system, during which time the town was divided into factions of two ideas, which were bitterly arrayed against each other. This contest had been going on for several years and the citizens had become so partisan that at the time this prosecution was commenced they immediately took sides contending either for the guilt or innocence of these defendants. This feeling permeated the entire County.[72]

On 17 April 1900, the aldermen formally notified the Grand Junction Water Company that "there was at the present time and for a considerable time previous . . . , in operation in the city of Grand Junction, a waterworks system owned and operated by the city." The communication continued, stating that

> no water was now being used or would be used by the city for fire hydrants, pipes, mains and pumps, from any other system than their own and that this was to be due notice to the Grand Junction Water Company of the

existence of this system of waterworks and of the stoppage of the use of the water, hydrants, pipes and pumps of any other system.[73]

The establishment and operation of a municipally owned water company climaxed almost two decades of political controversy in Grand Junction. That controversy reflected an emerging self-consciousness on the part of the community and a willingness to accept municipal responsibility. Initially, settlers had let the Grand Junction Town Company provide the community's water, but growing dissatisfaction led first to a carefully worded franchise to the Grand Junction Water Company and eventually to a desire to sever completely the relationship with any private company. The franchise signified a move away from the town company's control, yet at the same time an unwillingness to take on the responsibilities of municipal ownership. Then, dissatisfaction with the service and the quality of water provided by the water company caused residents, in time, to view municipal ownership as the only solution. In 1894, when Grand Junction voters approved a municipal system, they were also assuming a significantly greater responsibility for the continued vitality and growth of their community. So anxious were residents to assure the continuation of their town through the control of a municipal water system that they consented to build the system on the Grand River, which they knew supplied unsuitable water. They later supplanted the Grand with the purer Gunnison, but this river too suffered from the problems associated with spring runoffs. Within a decade, Grand Junction obtained mountain water, thus achieving both the goals of municipal ownership and quality water.[74]

The participation of Grand Junction settlers in the processes that resulted in municipal ownership may be measured in two ways: turnout on election day and turnover in officeholding. In general, participation in elections is related to issues, and citizens are more likely to go to the polls when they care strongly about those issues.[75] In Trempealeau County, Wisconsin, temperance was such an issue; in Kansas cattle towns, movements of moral reform generated high turnout; in Grand Junction, water provided the impetus. Whether the election centered on public debt or the makeup of the council, most settlers eligible to vote cast ballots. Turnout was very high in the elections that decided if the town would incur a public indebtedness: in three of four elections, more than 85 percent of those eligible voted. In one sense, the issue of municipal ownership rested in the hands of one-fifth of the adult population—property owners— because only they could participate in elections that put the town in debt. Viewing municipal ownership in such narrow terms, however, overlooks voter turnout at elections to determine aldermen. Although the men nominated for those positions were drawn from a specific segment of the community, annual elections provided all residents with the opportunity to change the board's composition— an opportunity they used. Turnout was high for the annual municipal election. In all but three years, more than half of Grand Junction's eligible voters cast ballots in naming municipal officeholders. The 1888 election aroused the least attention because there were no decisions: a slate for aldermen ran uncontested, and water was not yet a charged issue. On that occasion, fewer than 30 percent of the eligible voters cast ballots. Moreover, in most years, turnout for municipal elections was higher than for general, state, or county elections.[76]

Not only did the issues centering on water bring about high turnout on election day; they also encouraged turnover in office—a characteristic of the frontier. In mid-nineteenth-century Jacksonville, Illinois, few officeholders served a second term, although aldermen were more likely to be reelected than were other municipal officers. Similarly, most Trempealeau County, Wisconsin, officials occupied their posts for only a single term; but again, aldermen stood a better chance than others of reelection. Grand Junction aldermen experienced high turnover as well—fewer than one-third were reelected. Indeed, most never received a subsequent nomination, and among those who did the chances of election were slim. One historian has suggested that townspeople believed it their duty to serve on the council, but not for more than a term. Whether or not this was a widely shared view is impossible to weigh against voters' desire for change. However, the result, in pioneer community after community, was high turnover for aldermen.[77]

Turnover may have been high, but the job of alderman in frontier towns changed hands primarily among men who were married and held property—men with a stake in the community. Moreover, aldermen were engaged in business or in some skilled craft. In Grand Junction's first years of settlement, when the community was characterized by young single males, aldermen also tended to be young—

the median age for aldermen was about thirty—but even then, they were more likely to be married. Over time, aldermen were among the older men in the community—by the mid-1890s the median age had increased to forty—and virtually all were married.[78] Aldermen were always among the wealthiest community members: at least one-half were in the top deciles of property holders, though a few aldermen never reported any taxable wealth.

The significant turnout at the polls and turnover in officeholding in Grand Junction reflect widespread political participation. As settlers endeavored to build a community, they confronted problems that required political solutions. For some matters, such as organizing the town or electing school boards, resolutions were simple; but for others, especially the community water supply, solutions were more entangled. Such complex issues elicited greater response among settlers and encouraged more widespread participation, leading Merle Curti to conclude that "debate and differing opinion reveal a vital democracy." Robert R. Dykstra has seconded that conclusion, suggesting that "political factionalism was at least democracy's handmaiden."[79]

Political democracy emerged at the expense of the Grand Junction ·Town Company. Initially, the company made political decisions. It laid out the town, instigated the town's incorporation, and paid the mayor's expenses when he registered that incorporation. For the first few years, the company not only provided water for the town from its canal; it also argued persuasively against a permanent water facility. The company never had complete control, however, and by 1886 dissatisfaction with it had become a public issue. The 1888 election, which approved a franchise for the Grand Junction Water Company, was a rejection of the town company as well as a turn toward greater community control. By 1890 the town company had withdrawn from politics. The settlers of this frontier settlement had taken a few major steps, albeit not without some stumbling, toward building a community.

4 · POPULATION TURNOVER AND THE SOCIAL ARENA

"Some kind of organization which . . . affords both diversion and mental and social improvement."[1]

Like most nineteenth-century communities, Grand Junction experienced considerable turnover in its population. To be sure, enough of the earliest settlers were in the community in 1885 to form a Pioneer and Historical Society, and some were still there in 1900, but they constituted only about 13 percent of the original group. Grand Junction's dramatically high population turnover during its first two decades was a characteristic shared by most frontier communities. For a parallel period in Seattle's development, only 15.6 percent of the adult males persisted throughout a decade. With few exceptions, other recently settled western communities witnessed the emigration of at least two-thirds of their populations in the first decades. In Roseburg, Oregon, for example, only one-third of the adults counted in 1860 remained in 1870. The persistence rate was considerably lower in Jacksonville (from 1850 to 1860) and in the towns of Trempealeau county (1850–1860), where only one-quarter of the population took up permanent residence. Virtually no one continued to live in the mining towns of Grass Valley and Nevada City for even five years.[2]

Population turnover in young communities has been explained by such variables as wealth, property-holding, occupation, age, stage in the life cycle, and kin. Businessmen and professionals were more likely to remain than unskilled laborers, while younger and single men were more likely to emigrate than older and married ones. The presence of kin has also been shown to impede out-migration.[3]

Except for wealth, however, none of these factors significantly distinguished those families that would persist in Grand Junction from 1885 to 1900.[4] As Table 4 portrays, almost 80 percent of them reported taxable wealth, either real or personal property, to the Mesa County assessor in 1885. The other factor that distinguished those who stayed was participation in politics, in a church, or in a voluntary association (the "affiliate network"). Fully three-quarters of those families who remained from 1885 to 1900 contributed to activities beyond the home.

The prevailing notion among scholars who have studied recently settled communities in the nineteenth century is that within a highly transient frontier population, there developed a stable core, or what one historian has called those "with a stake in the community."[5] Certainly, the forty-eight families who persisted in pioneering in Grand Junction lend support to this assertion: they bought property, organized voluntary associations and churches, and ran for office. Significantly, however, they had matured along with Grand Junction and formed the community's "stable core." Like James W. Bucklin and his brother Harvey, in 1885 most of them had been young and many were single; by the turn of the century, they were middle-aged, owned real estate, and with three exceptions, were married and parents. It is incorrect, however, to assume that the 274 families not present in 1900 had remained only long enough to be counted by enumerator W. A. Marsh in June 1885. Still, although very few remained in Grand Junction during the entire period, more than half of the 322 individuals and families counted in the 1885 census settled for at least a year or two and some for as long as a dozen years, as Table 5 shows. The average tenure for the 1885 heads of family was more than five years.[6] For some, the "transients," this was undoubtedly true—that is, they were enroute when the census count was made. But at least 167 of these families considered taking up residence, for they joined voluntary associations and reported property to the county tax assessor.

Charles and Bessie Kent Mitchell headed one of these families. Both were pioneer settlers and had participated for years in such activities as the Masons and the Queen Isabella Study Group, a woman's club, when they moved to Ohio about two years before the 1900 census.[7] Similarly, Thomas B. Crawford had the features of someone who did not consider himself a transient and who worked to build the Grand Junction community. Crawford belonged

Table 4
Age, Life Cycle, Occupation, Wealth, and Networks of Emigrants and the Stable Core

	% among emigrants	% among stable core
A. Age of Family Head		
18–29	31.1	33.3
30–39	39.4	37.5
40–49	16.4	20.8
50+	13.1	8.3
B. Life Cycle Stage		
Single	53.6	37.5
Never married	(41.6)	(33.3)
Ever married	(12.0)	(4.2)
Married	46.4	62.5
No children	(11.3)	(20.8)
Children	(31.8)	(39.6)
Single parent	(3.3)	(2.1)
C. Occupation		
Business	12.8	16.7
Professional	5.1	10.4
Semiprofessional	9.5	6.3
Artisan	23.0	37.5
Trans./Comm.	10.9	6.3
Personal Service	7.7	4.2
Agriculture	12.4	8.3
Labor	10.6	6.3
Other	8.0	4.2
D. Property-holding		
No Property	55.1	20.8
Lower 50%	22.6	39.6
Upper 50%	22.3	39.6
E. Networks		
Affiliate	36.9	75.0
Kin	17.5	31.3
N	274	48

to several clubs and participated in the local militia, Company F, from its inception in 1882. When he left Grand Junction in 1894, it was to serve as adjutant general of Colorado's National Guard. All three of these people resided in Grand Junction for many years, but because they emigrated before the 1900 enumerator, Nannie Forry, made her rounds, their impact on the traditional measure of persistence is no greater than if they had stopped for a few days in June 1885.

Reliance on the census obscures the important role that individuals and families living in a community and participating in its activities (albeit for periods of short duration) played in the building of that community. The average length of residence for those who participated in some aspect of Grand Junction's community building was about eight years; yet the influence of these people is unperceived if only census data are utilized.[8] Many people were simply passing through Grand Junction. One-third of the 1885 families counted by W. A. Marsh were truly transient, as Table 5 points out. Except for their names on the census rolls, there is no evidence that they were ever in Grand Junction. The remainder, however, resided in the community for periods ranging from one to fifteen years. Thus, length of residence is more important in understanding the processes of community building than the fact of being present from one census to another.[9]

Several sources provide data for estimating length of residence and for distinguishing "transient" families from "resident" families (like the Mitchells and Crawford) who stayed long enough to join community organizations or to be listed at least once in the county assessor's records. Among these sources are newspaper accounts of local events, memberships lists for voluntary associations, and tax records.[10] Such sources also expose another shortcoming inherent in relying solely on the census: residents who were away on census day were not enumerated. For example, the Edwin Price family did not appear on the 1900 census rolls; either the family was out of town or Nannie Forry overlooked them (a highly unlikely occurrence because Forry and Edwin Price were both active in Republican politics). Whatever the reason for their omission from the census, both Edwin and Lola Price were residents. They lived in Grand Junction from 1882 to 1914, and during that time they remained active in the community. Publisher of the *Grand Junction News*, Edwin also

Table 5
Length of Residence for 1885 Families

	N	%	Cum. %
Resident 15 years	74	23.0	23.0
12	19	5.9	28.9
9	18	5.6	34.5
6	17	5.3	39.8
3	31	9.6	49.4
1	56	17.4	66.8
Transient	107	33.2	100.0
TOTAL	322		

Average length of residence:
all families = 5.44 years,
excluding transient = 8.14 years.

mounted several political campaigns and served a term on the town council. Lola helped organize the Women's Christian Temperance Union, the Queen Isabella Study Group, and the Grand Mesa Woman's Club. The same was true for at least two dozen other families living in Grand Junction. Although their names did not appear on the census rolls, they contributed to community building by their participation in its activities.

Except for wealth and participation, the forty-eight families, which formed what traditional techniques for studying population turnover would classify as Grand Junction's "stable core," were indistinguishable from the general population. The same cannot be said in comparing transient families (those who stayed only a short time, never bought property, or joined any organization) with resident families. Except for age of the head of family, transients and residents had little in common. As Table 6 demonstrates, transients were much more likely to be single than married, while the opposite was true of the residents.[11] Transient and resident families also differed in occupations. The former more frequently reported personal service, transportation and communication, and labor occupations; while the latter listed business, semiprofessional, or skilled employment. Kinship was another characteristic that set residents and transients apart. Like James and Harvey Bucklin, Julia and Addison McCune, and the Kents, Camerons, and Mitchells—families that stopped in

Table 6
Age, Life Cycle, Occupation, Wealth, and
Networks for Transient and Resident Families

	% among transients	% among residents
A. Age of Family Head		
18–29	28.8	32.8
30–39	37.3	40.2
40–49	21.2	14.7
50+	12.7	12.3
B. Life Cycle Stage		
Single	62.7	44.6
Never married	(43.2)	(38.7)
Ever married	(19.5)	(5.9)
Married	37.2	55.4
No children	(7.6)	(15.5)
Children	(25.4)	(37.5)
Single parent	(4.2)	(2.4)
C. Occupation		
Business	5.9	17.6
Professional	1.7	8.3
Semiprofessional	6.8	10.3
Artisan	22.9	26.5
Trans./Comm.	13.6	8.3
Personal Service	9.3	5.9
Agricultural	13.6	10.8
Labor	13.6	7.8
Other	12.7	4.4
D. Networks		
Kin	10.9	26.2
N	107	215

Grand Junction long enough to join a community organization or to acquire property—one in four of those who persisted had adult kin in the 1885 community when the census was enumerated; only one in ten transients could make a similar claim.

In general, the evidence for Grand Junction corroborates previous findings about population turnover: "within the dynamic flow of population a stable core persisted." However, the data for Grand Junction also suggest the need for a refinement in traditional thinking about persistence.[12] Rather than a division of the population into families that persisted (for a specified period) and those that departed, a three-part division provides a more accurate view. First, some proportion of the population was truly transient—that is en route—and only happened to be in Grand Junction at the time of the census enumeration. Second, a stable core existed. These people planned to stay and build the community, and they did. James W. Bucklin, Edwin and Lola Price, and Charles and Nettie McCarey typify Grand Junction's stable core. Their business interests and contributions to politics and voluntary associations enmeshed them in a commitment to the community. As they married and had children, their involvement with Grand Junction became even more rooted. The rest, the "interim residents," seem to have deliberated about staying. Like Charles and Bessie Mitchell, they purchased land, took part in the voluntary life of the settlement, and stayed for periods ranging from one to fourteen years. While the proportions in each category—transient, stable, and interim resident—undoubtedly vary in different settlements, the three-part typology portrays population turnover and community building more accurately than the traditional dichotomy based on persisters and nonpersisters. For Grand Junction, about one in every three families in the pioneer settlement were transient, and about one in four remained fifteen years to form the stable core. (See Table 5.)

Studying Grand Junction's population turnover not only permits a clearer understanding of who stayed to build the community; it also reveals how pioneers developed social institutions. In the past, as now, voluntary associations performed several functions both to individuals and to their communities. They ordered a community "by stressing," as one historian has claimed, "the unifying values its members shared." Individual associations provided members with a voice in dispersing power as well as a means of self-expression. Viewed collectively, voluntary associations furnished a means of incorporating heterogeneous concerns and interests within the community. Finally, such organizations often helped to integrate newcomers into the community.[13]

Grand Junction's pioneers were as quick to enter into a variety of voluntary associations as they were to establish their more formal political institutions. Like most recently settled areas, the first association in Grand Junction was a church. In summer 1882, the Methodist Episcopal Church South created a parish, and Rev. Father Isaac Witcher delivered a formal sermon on 9 October.[14] The establishment of other church groups followed swiftly. The newcomers' concern for their safety matched that for their souls in the recently opened territory, and in the autumn of 1882 they formed Company F, or the "Grand Valley Guards," a regiment consisting initially of thirty-four men: twelve officers and twenty-two privates. By the time of the state census in 1885, there were a total of twenty voluntary associations (six of them churches). Fifteen years later, at least seventy associations had been started in the settlement; although some convened only once or twice, others—about half—lasted for years and included many active members.[15]

The institution of voluntary associations was a critical aspect of community building, as important to the success of Grand Junction as its economic base and political structure. Voluntary associations facilitated interaction for residents and provided opportunities for the creation (and re-creation) of society. By 1885, 28.8 percent of the adult men had joined at least one organization. Women were less active during the pioneer years; only 6.5 percent belonged to any group, but they played an increasing role over time. At the turn of the century, women were as active as men in the voluntary community. Most settlers belonged to only one organization, but some were members of several groups.

A great deal of variation existed within the voluntary community, both among the ephemeral groups and the enduring ones. Following quickly after the formation of the Grand Valley Guards, pioneer men organized the Grand Army of the Republic (GAR) and the Masons, and women instituted a chapter of the Women's Christian Temperance Union. In 1884, settlers chartered four local organizations with economic and booster bases—the Board of Trade, the Mesa County Fair Association, the Mesa County Horticultural Society, and the Western Colorado Stock Grower's Association; in addition, they initiated the Independent Order of Odd Fellows, the Knights of Honor, and a Chautauqua Circle. The following year, they founded a library association and the Pioneer and Historical Society. By 1885 pioneers interested in participation might choose among fourteen organizations, each with a different raison d'être: fraternal, economic, reform, or educational. Not satisfied with these, settlers continued to form new associations. Many lasted only a few months, but others endured for years. Eight of the original fourteen still existed in 1900.[16]

The opportunity to participate in Grand Junction's associative society increased as the town matured. In the fifteen-year period between 1885 and 1900, settlers initiated fifty-six new organizations. The multiplication in associations was accompanied by changes in their character and purpose. Fraternal orders accounted for about one-third of the organizations that were active during the last few years of the nineteenth century. Except for the Masons, these groups provided insurance benefits as well as outlets for social activity.[17] Several occupationally specific organizations had also been initiated, and while most of these organizations provided insurance for members they also furnished opportunities to socialize. For example, the Brotherhood of Locomotive Engineers held an annual ball. At first, members of the Grand Valley Division journeyed to Salt Lake City for this event; but, in 1891, they inaugurated their own dance in Grand Junction. In particular (as will be explained later), the number of women's associations grew. Several auxiliaries to national fraternal organizations were chartered, as were two chapters of the General Federation of Women's Clubs.

The number of organizations increased over time, but only half of the seventy that had been started during Grand Junction's first two decades still functioned at the turn of the century. Although the transient nature of the frontier undoubtedly impeded the continuation for many social groups, those that endured were more likely to be affiliated with a national organization or to provide insurance benefits. Two-thirds of the thirty-three ephemeral organizations lacked either of these features. Most were strictly local in focus, although sometimes they were involved beyond the bounds of Grand Junction. A member of Grand Junction's Wheelmen won state recognition for his cycling speed. The Amazon Guards, a female drill team, competed statewide. The Western Slope Congress, a regional booster organization with an interest in the free coinage of silver, had chapters in most towns in western Colorado; the Grand Junction group was quite active between 1891 and 1894. Such clubs were formed around specific interests like music, sports, or erudition, but when these interests waned the clubs disbanded. Nevertheless, a variety of organizations provided ample opportunities for social participation.

Simply knowing that a sufficiently large number of organizations provided opportunities for membership does not answer questions about the nature of participation. What proportion of Grand Junction men belonged to any organization, and what socioeconomic characteristics distinguished joiners from nonjoiners? Were some men more active than others in voluntary associations? The same questions need to be asked of women's participation to discover whether there were significant differences between the social activities of men and women. (As with persistence, the following analysis of participation focuses on the family unit.)

By 1885 more than one-quarter of Grand Junction's adult male population had joined some organization. Male participants, like most heads of family, were in their twenties or thirties; and about one-half of them were single, as Table 7 shows. Because many early organizations were booster groups, merchants and professional men participated in greater numbers than artisans or men in transportation and communication. Participants also made a commitment to Grand Junction by purchasing property, and there was a relationship between participation in associative activities and taxable wealth. Not only did three-quarters of the participants hold property; most of them were in the upper half among property owners.

By the late 1890s the proportion of men who had joined Grand Junction's associative community had declined to 19.8 percent—about 10 percent fewer than in the community's formative years. Not only were proportionately fewer men participating, but their socioeconomic characteristics also became more distinct, as Table 8 illustrates. Joiners continued to be about the same age as nonjoiners, and like the general population, they now tended to be older, with only a few in their twenties. However, in life-cycle stage, occupation, and taxable wealth, participating men differed from their nonparticipating contemporaries, although the distinctions were not as precise as they had been fifteen years earlier. A greater percentage of the participating heads of family were married, and most had children. Businessmen, professionals, and semiprofessionals continued to be more active than others. At the same time, however, many more artisans and men in transportation and communication now contributed to the associative community. Wealth divisions were also less distinct: While most participants had taxable wealth in 1900, more than one-third reported no assets.

In general, these findings support historian Walter S. Glazer's conclusions that "associational activity was clearly correlated with

Table 7
Age, Life Cycle, Occupation, and Wealth of Male Participants, 1882 to 1885

	% in total population	% among participants	% among nonparticipants	minimum	moderate	maximum
A. Age						
18–29	31.4	31.1	31.5	34.6	34.0	17.6
30–39	39.1	42.2	37.9	50.0	40.4	35.3
40–49	17.1	13.3	18.5	7.7	12.8	23.5
50+	12.4	13.3	12.1	7.7	12.8	23.5
B. Life Cycle Stage						
Single	51.3	46.6	53.0	61.5	40.4	41.2
Never married	(40.4)	(43.3)	(39.2)	(57.7)	(38.3)	(35.3)
Ever married	(10.9)	(3.3)	(13.8)	(3.8)	(2.1)	(5.9)
Married	48.7	53.3	47.0	38.4	59.6	58.8
No children	(12.7)	(13.3)	(12.5)	(15.4)	(14.9)	(5.9)
Children	(32.9)	(38.9)	(30.6)	(19.2)	(44.7)	(52.9)
Single parent	(3.1)	(1.1)	(3.9)	(3.8)	(0.0)	(0.0)
C. Occupation						
Business	13.4	28.9	7.3	30.8	21.3	47.1
Professional	5.9	10.0	4.3	11.5	10.6	5.9
Semiprofessional	9.0	16.7	6.0	8.0	17.0	29.4
Artisan	25.2	18.9	27.6	11.5	25.5	11.8
Trans./Comm.	10.2	4.4	12.5	3.8	6.4	0.0
Personal Service	7.1	3.3	8.6	7.7	2.1	0.0
Agriculture	11.8	5.6	14.2	7.7	4.3	5.9
Labor	9.9	7.8	10.8	15.4	6.4	0.0
Other	7.5	4.4	8.6	3.8	6.4	0.0
D. Wealth						
No wealth	50.0	21.1	61.2	11.5	27.7	17.6
Lower 50%	25.3	28.9	23.7	34.6	29.8	17.6
Upper 50%	24.8	50.0	15.1	53.8	42.6	64.7
N	322	90	232	26	47	17

Table 8
Age, Life Cycle, Occupation, and Wealth of Male Participants, 1897 to 1900

	% in total population	% among participants	% among nonparticipants	minimum	moderate	maximum
A. Age						
18–29	14.3	7.3	16.1	7.9	8.5	0.0
30–39	31.0	31.5	30.9	31.5	33.8	22.2
40–49	30.8	36.5	29.4	36.0	33.8	50.0
50+	23.9	24.7	23.7	24.7	23.9	27.8
B. Life Cycle Stage						
Single	18.9	8.4	21.5	10.1	7.0	5.6
Never married	(13.3)	(3.9)	(15.7)	(3.4)	(4.2)	(5.6)
Ever married	(5.6)	(4.5)	(5.8)	(6.7)	(2.8)	(0.0)
Married	81.1	91.6	78.6	89.9	93.0	94.5
No children	(14.4)	(10.7)	(15.4)	(13.5)	(8.5)	(5.6)
Children	(60.7)	(80.9)	(55.7)	(76.4)	(84.5)	(88.9)
Single parent	(6.0)	(0.0)	(7.5)	(0.0)	(0.0)	(0.0)
C. Occupation						
Business	10.7	21.3	8.0	11.2	28.2	44.4
Professional	3.9	7.3	3.0	2.2	9.9	22.2
Semiprofessional	8.7	14.6	7.2	13.5	18.3	5.6
Artisan	20.0	19.7	20.1	23.6	16.9	11.1
Trans./Comm.	25.2	24.2	25.5	31.5	21.1	0.0
Personal Service	5.3	.6	6.5	1.1	0.0	0.0
Agriculture	4.7	3.4	5.0	3.4	2.8	5.6
Labor	11.6	2.8	13.7	3.4	1.4	5.6
Other	10.0	6.2	10.9	10.1	1.4	5.6
D. Wealth						
No wealth	61.2	38.8	66.8	47.2	38.0	0.0
Lower 50%	19.4	21.9	20.8	27.0	16.9	16.7
Upper 50%	19.3	39.3	12.5	25.8	45.1	83.3
N	900	178	722	89	71	18

... men in professional, managerial, and commercial positions" and that "there was a strong relationship between associational activity and property-holding." In Grand Junction, however, artisans and men in transportation and communication, especially white-collar workers and skilled railroaders, played an increasingly larger part in the associative community. By 1900, men in these occupations were participating in numbers roughly equivalent to those in all families; in 1885 they had been much less active. In part, union activity, explains this increased participation.[18] By the late 1890s, locomotive engineers, trainmen, and conductors had brotherhoods headquartered in Grand Junction, and similarly, carpenters and painters had unions. For railroad workers, increased activity also reflects the shift in personnel from laborers to locomotive engineers, conductors, and company officials like master mechanics, yardmasters, and clerks.[19] They were more likely than itinerant railroad laborers to see themselves as part of the community, and they joined the Masons, Odd Fellows, and Woodmen of the World. Five ran for public office. W. B. Lawrence, clerk for the Denver and Rio Grande, served a term as mayor, and Andrew McKinney, an engineer, acted as alderman. At the same time, the number of men with no wealth took a greater part in community activities; almost 40 percent had no taxable assets. The tendency toward more widespread participation—demonstrated by increased activity among Grand Junction's artisans and men in transportation and communication and by those without taxable wealth—suggests that class lines were not as rigidly drawn in frontier Grand Junction as they were in such longer-settled cities as Cincinnati.[20]

Levels of participation varied among the men in Grand Junction's voluntary community. Some belonged to many groups and held several positions, while others joined only one organization and never achieved an office. About one-fifth of the participants in the formative years (from 1882 to 1885) could be classified as "maximum" activists. Like Richard D. Mobley, who helped in organizing the GAR and the Masons and campaigned for mayor, these men joined several groups, held a variety of offices, and frequently received attention in the newspaper. About half were "moderate" activists—that is, they belonged to more than one organization or held an office or two. Typical was J. H. Ackerman, who held memberships in the IOOF and was named twice as an officer in that group. The remainder, "minimum" activists, belonged to only one group and never held an office. Regardless of their level of activity (as Table 7 demonstrates), the men who participated in Grand Junction's pioneer period were similar to one another in age, life-cycle stage, occupation, and wealth.[21]

By the turn of the century the level of participation changed, as did the socioeconomic characteristics of the participants. About the same number of men were maximum activists (as Table 8 shows), but because twice as many men now participated, this clique of multiple joiners and officeholders now comprised only one-tenth of the participants. About two-thirds were businessmen or professionals, and they were among the most wealthy: all reported some wealth, and more than three-quarters ranked in the upper 50 percent. Wendall P. Ela, businessman and mayor, was among Grand Junction's most active citizens. Ela belonged to the Board of Trade, the Camera Club, the Academy of Science, and the Masons. Attorney James W. Bucklin, member of the Masons, pursued his political career, and in 1900 he successfully campaigned for the state senate. Businessmen also made up the largest percentage of the moderate activists. Other moderates were semiprofessionals, although artisans and men in transportation and communication were about as active. Wealth differentiated participants even more finely. Minimum activists split about evenly between those with wealth and those without.

Only the most general comparison can be made between the levels of participation in Grand Junction and other locales. Although scholars of the nineteenth-century frontier have made participation a primary topic of study, their focus has been on power or leadership. Often such examinations ignore minimal participants and thereby leave part of the story untold. Idiosyncratic definitions of participation also hamper comparisons. Finally, while there is consensus that participation relates to such socioeconomic characteristics as wealth, occupation, and age, there is little consistency in categorizing these variables.[22]

Nevertheless, while precise comparisons cannot be drawn, the broad conclusions of these studies may be examined for similarities. Taken together, the moderate and maximum participants in Grand Junction approximate the "leaders," as defined by Curti, Alcorn, and Doyle.[23] Curti found that in Trempealeau County, throughout the period from 1860 to 1880, most leaders were men in their thirties who had more property than the general population, even though younger men dominated the population at large. Subsequent studies confirm that leaders were wealthier and older than those they led. In both periods examined for Grand Junction—1882 to 1885 and 1897 to 1900—leaders similarly held more taxable property than the population at large, but they were no older.[24]

Findings about leaders' occupations are not so easily generalized, however. To be sure, professionals and businessmen dominated leadership positions regardless of study site, including Grand Junction. In Trempealeau County, for example, leadership before 1860 mirrored the general population; after 1860 professionals and businessmen displaced farmers, although their proportions in the total population did not change significantly. Because of the problems surrounding occupation categorization, the role of skilled workers is not so clear. In Grand Junction, artisans and men in transportation and communication never commanded leadership positions in proportion to their numbers in the population. Moreover, in that community the percentage of artisans who were leaders declined, while the fraction of men in transportation and communication increased, again indicating the importance of the railroad.[25]

Comparisons about the activity level among leaders are equally difficult to draw because common criteria for distinguishing major from minor leaders have not been utilized.[26] However, regardless of how those in leadership positions have been categorized, one conclusion emerges: There was a very active elite among the leaders. These men held positions in several types of organizations, and in general, they were older, wealthier, and involved in commercial, professional, or semiprofessional occupations. Except for age, Grand Junction's most active men fit the criteria for this elite. In both periods analyzed for Grand Junction, the men who participated were no older than the general population, regardless of level of activity.

Men's participation in late nineteenth-century Grand Junction changed as the settlement matured. A greater proportion of men joined clubs during the first few years than in the later period. For women, the pattern of participation was reversed. Only eleven women (6.5 percent) engaged in associative activity in 1885, but (as will be explained shortly) women's participation increased as Grand Junction developed. By the last years of the century, the proportion of women involved in associations almost tripled. Ten of the several organizations started were exclusively female, and in three others most members were women.

Only two organizations had women members in the early years—

the WCTU and the Chautauqua. The eleven female participants tended to be under the age of thirty, as were most women in the community. Like Lola Price and Emma Mobley, they were married and had children. Of the three who were single, two were teachers residing with married sisters, and the third, Emma Kent, lived with her parents. The largest percentage of women participants lived in families where the head (husband, father, or brother-in-law) earned his living in some semiprofessional pursuit. As Table 9 shows, none of the women were related to men employed in personal service, transportation and communication, or general labor. More than half came from families that were in the upper-wealth decline.

By the turn of the century the proportion of women participating had increased threefold, with about as many women involved in Grand Junction's social activities as men. Table 9 points out that those active in the later period tended to be somewhat older than nonjoiners: almost half were in their thirties, while among nonactivists only one-third were in that age group. Married women with children joined in much greater numbers than they had in the earlier period. Twenty-two unmarried women were also active: three were heads of family; three others were either the mother or mother-in-law of the family head; twelve were daughters (nine employed); three were boarders (all employed); and one was a servant. More than half of the active women lived in families in which the head was employed in business or some professional or semiprofessional pursuit, while one-third were married to artisans or men engaged in transportation and communication. At the same time, women participants were now less likely to come from the wealthier families. More than one-quarter of them resided in families with no taxable wealth in 1900.

The tremendous increase in women's participation reflects the expansion of opportunities for them in the late nineteenth century in organizations such as women's clubs and auxiliaries to fraternities.[27] The Queen Isabella Study Group was one of the first "women's clubs" formed in Grand Junction. Organized in 1892, its "purpose was exciting the interest of women . . . in all matters pertaining to the Women's Department of the [Chicago] World's Fair." "The World's Fair . . . had stimulated an interest in foreign countries," a club historian explained, "so preliminary studies were undertaken, and later, the fortunate women who had visited the Fair reported their impressions." Members reorganized in 1895 "to keep abreast

Table 9
Age, Life Cycle, Family Occupation, and Wealth of Female Participants, 1882 to 1885 and 1897 to 1900

		1882–1885			1897–1900	
	% in total population	% among participants	% among nonparticipants	% in total population	% among participants	% among nonparticipants
A. Age						
15–29	51.8	40.0	52.7	33.0	17.4	36.4
30–39	32.4	30.0	32.6	36.6	46.1	34.5
40+	15.8	30.0	14.6	30.4	36.5	29.1
B. Life Cycle Stage						
Single	7.1	30.0	7.5	3.6	3.8	4.3
Never married	(7.1)	(30.0)	(7.5)	2.0	(3.8)	(2.4)
Ever married	(0.0)	(0.0)	(0.0)	(1.6)	(0.0)	(1.9)
Married	92.9	70.0	92.4	96.4	96.2	95.7
No children	(24.3)	(20.0)	(24.5)	(17.6)	(12.0)	(18.1)
Children	(62.7)	(50.0)	(61.6)	(71.7)	(78.2)	(70.3)
Single parent	(5.9)	(0.0)	(6.3)	(7.1)	(6.0)	(7.3)
C. Occupation of household head						
Business	14.8	30.0	13.8	12.3	29.8	8.7
Professional	5.3	10.0	5.0	4.2	7.4	3.6
Semiprofessional	11.2	40.0	9.4	9.7	18.2	8.0
Artisan	26.0	10.0	27.0	21.0	18.2	21.6
Trans./Comm.	9.5	0.0	10.1	30.7	14.9	34.0
Personal Service	7.1	0.0	7.5	5.5	3.3	6.0
Agriculture	14.2	10.0	14.5	5.4	4.1	5.6
Labor	5.9	0.0	6.3	11.1	4.1	12.6
Other	5.9	0.0	6.3	0.0	0.0	0.0
D. Wealth						
No wealth	39.6	10.0	41.5	58.4	27.1	64.8
Lower 50%	30.2	20.0	30.8	21.0	26.3	19.9
Upper 50%	30.2	70.0	27.7	20.6	46.6	15.3
N	169	11	158	762	133	629

of the times," renaming themselves the Twentieth-Century Club and limiting membership to thirty-five. They joined the Colorado Federation of Women's Clubs in 1896, and the national federation the following year.[28] Meanwhile, other women, some of them former members of the Queen Isabella Study Club, formed the Grand Mesa Woman's Club. Like the Twentieth-Century Club, this organization belonged to both the state and national federations.[29] In general, women's clubs were committed to community improvement, and in Grand Junction that commitment resulted in a public library, something townspeople had talked about for years. Several groups had tried, without success, to muster financial support for a public library. In 1898, however, the two women's clubs jointly formed the Women's Library Association of Grand Junction and established a public library.[30]

Several auxiliaries to fraternal associations were also inaugurated in the mid-1890s. The Daughters of Rebekah (auxiliary to the Odd Fellows) and the Rathbone Sisters of America (Knights of Pythias) began in 1895, followed by the Daughters of Pocahontas (Improved Order of Redmen) and Women of Woodcraft (Woodmen of the World) in 1898.[31] In Colorado specifically, increased participation also represents the results of the 1893 suffrage amendment. Even before women were fully franchised they took part in Colorado politics. As a result of a provision in the state constitution of 1876, women could vote in school-related elections and hold school-board positions. In 1893, suffragist Carrie Chapman toured Colorado to muster support for women's rights, and in Grand Junction she helped in organizing the Woman Suffrage League in September of that year. Jessie Caswell was president of the group, and the following February she was named to head the Mesa County Political and Social Science Club—a group dedicated to the "systematic study of political economy and civil government with a view of educating and fitting the ladies for the duties and rights of equal citizenship."[32] Caswell remained active in politics, and in 1898, she was nominated on the state Republican ticket for regent of the university.

Perhaps because most studies of participation have been interested in power and have perceived women as powerless, little is known about their role in community building. Nevertheless, "letters and reminiscences," historian Julie Roy Jeffrey points out, ". . . attest to the early and spirited efforts of pioneer women to create their social world." At first, "women made their major contributions to and through their families." Later on, "women's social contacts multiplied."[33] The data from Grand Junction support Jeffrey's assertion. In 1885 few women had the time to join, much less initiate, formal organizations: those who did were members of wealthier families, which presumably freed them from many of the demands of starting new homes. By the turn of the century more women could turn their attention to activities outside the home. Thus, the increased participation of women in voluntary associations also provides a measure of transition. For women, at least, small-town Grand Junction provided more widespread opportunity than had the pioneer settlement.

In the pioneer community, women's involvement in voluntary associations was so narrow that any discussion of levels of participation or leadership is pointless, but by the late 1890s a hierarchy emerged. Like men, some women belonged to only one organization, while others joined several groups and held elective offices. About half of the women were moderate participants like Nettie McCarey, who belonged to the Rebekah and held office in that organization at one time. McCarey had resided in Grand Junction since her marriage in 1886, but the duties associated with beginning her family kept her at home. Not until her younger son was seven did she join the Rebekah.[34] Few women (6.7 percent) qualified as maximum participants. One was Sarah J. Telford, who focused her energies on temperance and led both the local and district organizations. In addition, she twice served as state president of the WCTU. Even though a hierarchy of involvement developed among women by the late 1890s, socioeconomic characteristics did not distinguish that hierarchy. Regardless of level of participation, women joiners were very similar in age, life-cycle stage, and family occupation and wealth.

For women and men, then, participation in late nineteenth-century Grand Junction underwent change as the settlement matured. The opportunity to participate remained open as the number and variety of organizations increased. During the first few years a large proportion of men took part in associative activity, but that percentage decreased over time. Although exact comparisons cannot be drawn with other frontier studies, the findings for Grand Junction support the notion that participation was linked to occupation and wealth. While artisans and men in transportation and communication may not have played major roles in Grand Junction's voluntary community, they nonetheless increased their level of participation by 1900 beyond what it had been during the early years of settlement. Similarly, the voluntary community expanded to include more women by the turn of the century; more organizations were available and almost as many women as men participated. In contrast to the earlier period, there was increased participation from women whose husbands were in personal service, transportation and communication, or skilled labor. At the same time, more than one-quarter of the women who joined came from families with no taxable wealth.

Thus, in many ways, the possibilities to participate in Grand Junction's associative community had increased by the turn of the century. To be sure, positions of leadership in men's organizations consolidated in the hands of wealthier businessmen and professionals, but opportunities to take part in the associative life of the community remained open. Moreover, there was a relationship between participation in community activities and persistence, although the direction of that relationship is debatable: Did pioneers participate because they remained, or did they remain because they participated? Voluntary associations also facilitated the entry of newcomers into the community and seemingly encouraged them to stay. As the next chapter points out, that participation provided a basis for greater social intimacy—what one contemporary author called "knowing the details of one another's lives."[35]

5 · SOCIAL INTERACTION: *Inside and Outside the Family*

...*"knowing the details of one another's lives."*[1]

Pioneers in Grand Junction, as elsewhere on the frontier, faced uncertainty as they began new lives and a new community. Would they be able to make a living? Would they be able to build schools and churches? Would their community develop a strong economic base? Would Grand Junction attract more families, or would settlers pass over their community in favor of some other location? Pioneers confronted these uncertainties directly as they laid the economic, political, and social cornerstones for their community.

In convincing the Denver and Rio Grande Railway to locate its maintenance shops in Grand Junction, pioneer town builders took a major step toward ensuring their community's position in the regional economic hierarchy. Their gradual recognition of the relationship between adequate water and community development also diminished uncertainty about Grand Junction's chances for success. However, they were not focused solely on making a living or promoting their community. Pioneers also attended to social concerns. Foremost among these concerns were family relationships, but opportunities also emerged for extrafamilial social interaction—politics, churches, and voluntary associations.

Family relationships enhanced stability in the nascent community. Although most men were single, many had migrated with relatives. Thus, during Grand Junction's pioneer period, some settlers could look to kin for emotional support and companionship. Social interaction outside the family also helped to strengthen the frontier community as pioneers became acquainted. For example, everyone needing flour, sugar, coffee, or other supplies must have entered Charles Mitchell's general store. Those people who purchased town lots for businesses or homes negotiated with George A. Crawford, his nephew Thomas B. Crawford, or Monroe Allison. If they hired builders, they probably looked to J. H. Ackerman and J. J. Lumsden.

Interaction did not end with basic necessities. When pioneers acted in concert—as they did when they elected the first school board in June 1882, when they incorporated the town three weeks later, or when they founded churches and voluntary associations—they also came to know one another. Pioneers celebrated life's crucial events—marriages, a child's christening, or a funeral—and they asked new friends to witness those events. Through these encounters, pioneers came to "know the details of one another's lives." Such relationships, social networks based on kinship and contacts outside the family, helped pioneers in confronting the uncertainties of frontier life. As Grand Junction developed, relationships based on kinship became more widespread as a result of marriages and the immigration of relatives. Relationships outside the family also tied the community together.[2]

Historians have long believed that migration to the frontier usually took place in conjugal units comprised of husband, wife, and children. Recent research has modified this assumption and suggested that migration was a more complex phenomenon. In a study of California mining camps, for example, Ralph Mann found evidence of kin relationships among the single males who responded to the gold rush. In Jacksonville, Illinois, 28 percent of the adult men in 1850 could count another adult male in the community—father, son, or cousin—as kin. Proportions were even higher in frontier Seattle, where "fully half of [the] earliest settlers had kin nearby."[3] For pioneer Grand Junction in 1885, about one-third of the adult settlers had relatives in the community.

Most studies of kinship have focused on men because the U. S. Bureau of the Census did not precisely identify the various relationships in the household until 1880. That focus upon men has resulted in an unbalanced view of migration, leading one historian to assert that in the frontier years "kin relationships were usually male because men so often determined the move and the settlement."[4] But changes in the questions asked by census enumerators in 1880 (and thereafter) facilitate the study of female kinship ties, and as Table 10 shows, women in pioneer Grand Junction were more likely to have female relatives than the men were to have male kin.[5] Fifteen years later, the proportion of females related to females was about the same as the figure for men. It seems likely, therefore, that in solely examining male relationships the importance of kin has been underestimated.

Other family relationships have also been obscured by focusing on males. A man living with his mother obviously would have counted her as kin, and presumably he would have also viewed his mother-in-law as a relative, particularly if she lived in his household.[6] A more illuminating definition of kinship includes any adult relative, regardless of gender, living inside or outside the residential household. It also embraces blood relatives and in-laws. Viewing kinship in this manner reveals that for pioneer Grand Junction, a community made up mostly of single males, about one in five families (19.6 percent) could turn to some adult kin in the community. By 1900 that proportion had increased to one-third (32.7 percent) because families played a larger role in the community. In addition, marriages that occurred between the early 1880s and 1900 blended families together and extended the kinship network.

Grand Junction's kinship network was simple in the pioneer period. Most people had only one relative in the community, and usually (62.7 percent) that relative was an adult sibling. Some, like Thomas and Gaylord Murray or Addison and Julia McCune, lived together; while others, like James and Harvey Bucklin or Morris Haggerty and Kate Haggerty Vaughn, lived apart. Another common

Table 10
Kin Relationships for Men and Women, 1885 and 1900

	1885		1900	
	men	women	men	women
Relative of same sex	19.0%	22.3%	28.8%	27.4%
Relative of opposite sex	8.9	18.3	24.8	30.3
Relative of either sex	27.9	40.6	53.6	57.7
N	406	197	1,215	993

relationship involved parents and their adult children. Sometimes, parents lived with their children (16.4 percent); other times, the children had married and lived nearby with their own families (6.3 percent); most often, however, adult children resided with their parents (22.3 percent). James and Amanda Kent had three adult daughters in Grand Junction; Emma was still living at home, but Bessie and Celia were married and residing in their own homes. Mary Chenowith's family contained a teenage son as well as her widowed daughter, Bessie, and Bessie's two children. However, relationships were not limited to siblings or parents and children. Thomas B. Crawford was the nephew of the town's founder, and his wife Emma's brother, Monroe, also resided in the community.[7]

Kinship played an important role in the processes of migration and settlement, and as the community matured the kinship network became broader and more complex. To be sure, sibling relationships were still common in 1900, and a few single adult siblings resided together. Other single adults resided with married brothers or sisters, and still others lived nearby in separate families. As in 1885, parents and adult children continued to live together; in 1900 almost half of the families (48.8 percent) had adult children at home.[8] More importantly, by 1900, as a result of marriages, the arrival of relatives, and the continued settlement of families, several of the simple relationships had evolved into what may be called "clans."

The marriages that occurred during the fifteen years between censuses not only altered the living arrangements for many couples, but expanded the kinship network as well.[9] The Murray brothers, for example, had both wed; Thomas married Bessie Chenowith Griffiths, and Gaylord wed Laura Bomgarden, a woman whose family arrived after 1885. Laura's sister married A. A. Miller, thereby linking three of the community's earliest settlers. Both of the Bucklin brothers were married; Harvey wed Maggie Lumsden, sister of pioneer settler J. J. Lumsden, and James married a woman from a nearby community.

Families with children of marriageable age also expanded their kinship bonds as these young people wed. The Kent's daughter, Emma, married Addison McCune; and another daughter, Celia Campbell, remarried after the death of her husband. Their third daughter, Bessie, and her husband Charles Mitchell remained in Grand Junction until the late 1890s. In addition, this clan now included Addison's spinster sister, Julia, and the McCune's niece living with Julia. The Fletcher family also changed as the older children wed or moved away from home. Ollie and George, both youngsters when the family settled in Grand Junction in 1883, were married and had children, and their younger twin brothers had established a separate household that included a boarder. Moreover, the parents, Robert and Ellen, were not living together in 1900. Robert lodged with Gaylord and Laura Murray, and Ellen lived with their fifth child, now a teenager, who had been born in Grand Junction. Parent's households contracted, then, while their kinship networks were enriched and expanded.

Immigration to Grand Junction by other family members also helped to enlarge and strengthen the kinship network. James and Harvey Bucklin's brother Alvin, a traveling salesman, visited Grand Junction in 1882 and purchased property. In 1890, he settled permanently in the town. In addition, the Bucklin's niece, Thusa Glassford, was now living in Grand Junction with her husband. Neither the Kents nor the Bucklins were the largest clan, however. That distinction went to the Crawfords, even though George Crawford, the first member of the family to take up residence, never married. From the outset, he had encouraged his relatives in Pennsylvania to follow him, and he had taken up land in their names. Several accepted his invitation. Thomas, a nephew who was the first to arrive in 1882, accepted a position with the town company. Thomas's sister Charlotte (Lottie) and brother Will soon arrived, and they were followed in the late 1880s by Charles B. Rich and John G. McKinney, other nephews. Then, in the fall of 1890, George Crawford's widowed sister (and Charles's mother), Josephine Rich, located in the town, bringing her other child, Jodie. Jodie recounted the reunion to a cousin who was still in Pennsylvania.

> When we got out of the street car at the Hotel [,] Charlie and John were at the door. . . . Lottie came around soon after we had breakfast. She and I then started out to view the town. We soon met Tommy and his wife. . . . After we left them we met Johnny C and while we were talking to him Will came up and then John. There were five cousins standing on the street corner talking.[10]

Josephine Rich was so taken with Grand Junction that she also promoted relocation. Three months after her arrival, her niece Lottie reported to a correspondent in the East that "she will have the whole family out here before long."[11] When Josephine and Jodie arrived, Thomas, Lottie, Will, and John were already married—thus further expanding the Crawford clan. Both Charles and Jodie wed before the end of the century, and Charles's marriage to the niece of H. T. DeLong, another longtime resident, bound those two pioneer families together.

Social interaction in Grand Junction reached beyond the family to include such formally organized groups as the Women's Christian Temperance Union and Grand Army of the Republic (with their elected officers and regular meetings). The social milieu also included political and religious affiliations.[12] A school board election on 1 June 1882 marked the community's first political exercise, and three weeks later, town incorporation mobilized participation. These caucuses not only addressed concerns of early settlers, but also identified men interested in public office. More than one-third of the men who voted for incorporation would later mount political campaigns. At about the same time, settlers also formed their first churches, and while the primary function of churches was religious observation, congregations also provided opportunities for social interaction.

Participation in activities beyond the family facilitated social intimacy, providing residents with the chance to know one another better. Those who joined more than one organization obviously increased their familiarity with others. Moreover, they connected the associations in which they participated and acted as intermediaries—or "bridges," as one historian has labeled them—between members in different organizations.[13] Taken together, these activities, based on voluntary associations, political caucuses, and churches, form Grand Junction's "affiliate network." Like the kinship network, the affiliate network provided settlers with the opportunity to know one another, and it helps to explain community building.

Grand Junction's affiliate network developed within a few years of settlement. In addition to the fourteen more formal voluntary associations (discussed in Chapter 4), the network contained six churches: the Methodist Episcopal, Catholic, Baptist, Methodist Episcopal South, Christian, and Presbyterian. It also afforded several opportunities for political interaction since elections were scheduled twice each year, in the spring to elect municipal officers, and in the autumn to choose county, state, or national officials. All of the candidates for municipal office were Grand Junction residents, as were some who sought county positions. By 1885 about three dozen local men had participated in the affiliate network by campaigning for public office.

The affiliate network included one-third of the families in the pioneer period. It was highly cohesive because so many men belonged to the Board of Trade and also participated in other organizations. The board's roster included half of the membership of the Odd Fellows, the GAR, and the Knights of Honor. The board had very strong ties to politics as well; eleven of its thirty-three members campaigned for public office. The Board of Trade was not the only organization with overlapping memberships. Six members of the GAR also belonged to the Pioneer and Historical Society; four members of the Knights of Honor participated in the Chautauqua Circle; and several Knights were also associated with the WCTU. Even when no direct ties existed between organizations, the pivotal organization—the Board of Trade—served as the nucleus of the affiliate network. No one, for example, joined both the Knights of Honor and the Masons, but C. W. Burris, who belonged only to the Knights of Honor, and W. J. Quinn, who belonged only to the Masons, had access to one another because they both had lodge brothers in the Board of Trade. Therefore, any family belonging to just one organization was potentially linked to many others. Figure 3, a sociogram, displays the affiliate network for pioneer Grand Junction.[14]

Active families served as the intermediaries in Grand Junction's network of affiliations. J. A. and Louisa Layton were one of those families. He belonged to the Board of Trade and the Pioneer Society. Layton was a volunteer fireman and helped in founding the GAR. Both of the Laytons belonged to the Chautauqua Circle and the Methodist Episcopal Church. Closely tied to the Laytons were Richard D. and Emma Mobley. Instrumental in founding the town, Mobley was eligible for the Pioneer and Historical Society. With Layton, he helped to organize the GAR, and he and his wife also belonged to the same church as the Laytons. Mobley ran for mayor, and Emma Mobley participated in the WCTU. A. A. Miller was the person most involved in the pioneer community. He belonged to the Board of Trade and the Odd Fellows, drilled with Company F, ran for the town council, and joined the Pioneer and Historical Society. These affiliations provided Miller with direct interaction with eighty other families. The Mobleys, the Laytons, and Miller, all of whom were active in several groups, were the adhesive of a tight network.

Active pioneers also connected the less involved to the affiliate

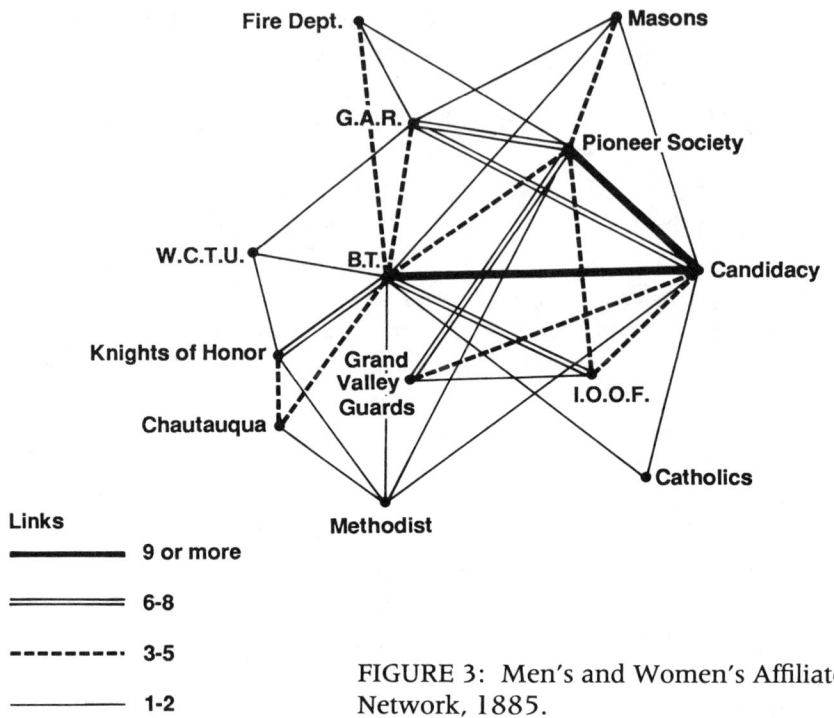

FIGURE 3: Men's and Women's Affiliate Network, 1885.

network. Catholics, for example, tended to participate solely in their church, in part because church guidelines prohibited them from joining any organization with a secret ritual. Yet Catholics were not isolated entirely from social interaction; one of their members, John Hynes, belonged to the Board of Trade and was politically active, and he was one of the few men elected to the town council more than once. Although Hynes participated in only three activities—the Catholic Church, the Board of Trade, and public office—these afforded him contact with sixty-four families. Hynes served as a bridge between other Catholics and the affiliate network. Thus, someone like Felix Toupaine, who settled in Grand Junction with his wife and five children in 1883 and who never joined any activity outside his church, was indirectly linked to more than fifty families beyond the dozen Catholic families with whom he worshiped. Moreover, because Hynes belonged to the Board of Trade, which had members in every other organization, Toupaine was no more than three steps away from any family in the affiliate network.

Fifteen years later, the affiliate network was both much larger and less cohesive, although the proportion of families involved remained relatively unchanged. There were more voluntary organizations; five additional churches; and the opportunity to be a candidate for local, county, and state office had increased significantly, especially in the wake of the disputes over water.[15] More Grand Junction residents campaigned at the state level. The Prohibition party nominated William A. Rice for secretary of state and William A. Marsh for treasurer in 1898. That same year, the Republicans named Jessie Caswell, organizer of the Grand Junction Woman Suffrage League, as their candidate for the University of Colorado's Board of Regents. Two years later, Grand Junction residents were candidates for almost every office, including presidential elector.

The affiliate network was less cohesive at the turn of the century than it had been fifteen years earlier. This is, in part, a result of population increase. However, the proliferation of organizations is also responsible. Although overlapping memberships continued to be one characteristic of participation, no group now fused the affiliate network as the Board of Trade had done during the first years of settlement. The Masons were one of the largest organizations, and many of its members belonged to other groups (as Figure 4 illustrates). The exclusiveness of that organization, however, prohibited it from providing as common a forum for social interaction as the Board of Trade had done earlier.

Although the affiliate network was now less cohesive, several families served to tie the community together. A. R. and Emma Wadsworth were one such household. Together, they joined the Daughters of Rebekah, and both were active in politics. A. R. served two terms on the town council, and when women were franchised in Colorado, Emma helped in organizing the Political Social Science Club. Emma's activity in the Grand Mesa Woman's Club earned her the opportunity to attend the national convention of the General Federation of Women's Clubs in 1897. She later served as a delegate to the state convention. Town mayor Wendell P. Ela and his wife Lucy were also very interactive. He held memberships in the Masons, the Academy of Science, and the Camera Club; she helped to initiate the Queen Isabella Study Group and was active in the Children's Home Society—an organization to aid "homeless and friendless children."[16] James Bucklin must have been among the most well known men in the community, although he joined only the Masons. Instead,

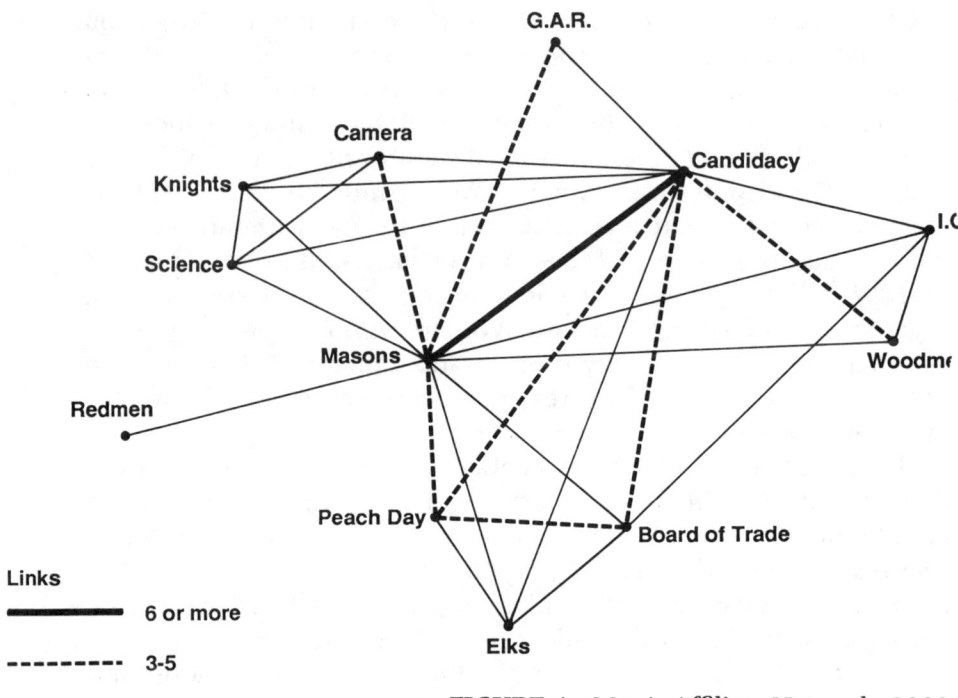

FIGURE 4: Men's Affiliate Network, 1900

he directed most of his attention to politics, campaigning several times and serving as mayor, state representative, and state senator. His wife, Mary, belonged to the Twentieth-Century Woman's Club.

Clearly, women's groups played a more important role in the affiliate network by the late 1890s, partly because more women's groups were created, but especially because women increased their participation in voluntary organizations and politics. In many families, in fact, the woman was the sole participant in community affairs. Ella Belle Ackerman was one of the more active women in the community. She belonged to the Rebekah, the Women's Relief Corps, the Women of Woodcraft, and the Rathbone Sisters.

Two cliques developed among women's affiliations. At the heart of one was the Daughters of Rebekah, a women's auxiliary to the Independent Order of Odd Fellows. Members of the Rebekah also belonged to the Women's Relief Corps, the Women of Woodcraft, and the WCTU. At the center of the other clique were the two chapters of the General Federation of Women's Clubs: the Twentieth-Century Woman's Club and the Grand Mesa Woman's Club.

Members of the women's club clique were also found in the Children's Home Society and in the Art League. Figure 5 portrays these cliques.

Family wealth and the husband's occupation distinguished one clique from the other. Among the dozen women who belonged to the clique centering on the women's clubs, ten (83.3 percent) were in the upper 50-percent wealth category, and half had husbands in business. None lived in families where the husbands were artisans or employed in transportation and communication, much less as laborers. The clique that centered on the Rebekah, on the other hand, had a broader socioeconomic base. About one-quarter of the women who joined one of these organizations resided in families that reported no wealth (26.1 percent), and their husbands found employment in a wider range of pursuits including artisanship and laboring.

The estrangement between women's organizations did not mean that the community's affiliate network no longer functioned; rather, the network was more characterized by nuance. The cliques, moveover, were not absolutely unconnected. A common project, like the library, might bridge the distance. (See Figure 5.) On the other hand, men's organizations were never as segregated as women's. Although no woman who joined the Women of Woodcraft, for example, ever

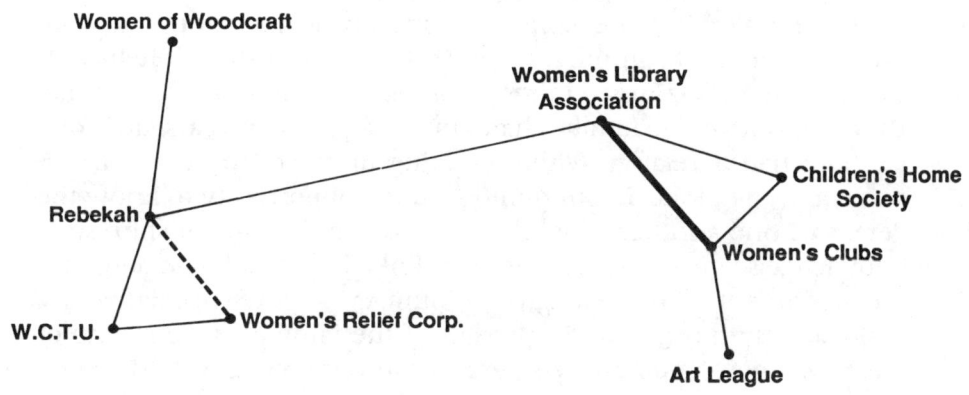

FIGURE 5: Women's Affiliate Network, 1900

participated in either the Twentieth-Century or Grand Mesa Woman's Club, her husband might belong to both the Woodmen of the World and the Masons. The only male organizations that might be called elite were the Western Slope Science Club and the Camera Club, but their memberships numbered so few that they played no significant role in the affiliate network.

The affiliate network facilitated the entry of newcomers into Grand Junction's social milieu because it introduced newcomers to a host of families.[17] Within two years of settling, Avery and Martha Newton, for example, were linked to more than 140 other families. The Newtons joined the Presbyterian Church, and Avery was a Mason. Martha belonged to the Grand Mesa Woman's Club and, with Emma Wadworth, served as a delegate to the women's clubs state convention. In joining three of Grand Junction's larger organizations, the Newtons were immediately enmeshed in the community's social interaction. Similarly, David and Isadora Clark joined the Daughters of Rebekah about three years after moving to Grand Junction. David later became a member of the Odd Fellows and the Masons. By 1900 Clark was so well known that he earned a nomination for alderman.

The affiliate network intermingled the social and political lives of the residents of Grand Junction. In the early years, as well as at the turn of the century, about one-third of the community's families belonged to some organization. While most of them joined only one such group, they were linked to others in the settlement by those who were multiple joiners. The kinship network also helped to integrate settlers into the pioneer community. Kin relationships were present from the beginning, when O. D. and Milt Russell helped in staking the first claim, and those relationships multiplied over time. By 1885, one in five families had kin nearby; fifteen years later, one in three had a relative within walking distance. In all, about 45 percent of the pioneer community had the opportunity to know the details of one another's lives.[18] For those bonded by kinship, such knowledge seemed assured; for those linked in the affiliate network, the determination of the degree of intimacy is more speculative. By 1900 slightly more than 55 percent of the families were in one of these two networks, and 10 percent were involved in both. Such intermingling supports the commonly held notion that small communities are places where "everyone knows everyone else." For recently settled communities like Grand Junction, that intermingling lent a sense of belonging.

CONCLUSION
Grand Junction and the Genesis of the Small Town

"Of Taylorville, where I grew up and was married, the most distinguishing thing was that there was nothing to distinguish it from a hundred other towns in Ohianna."[1]

Grand Junction's evolution from pioneer settlement to small town resembled that of other nineteenth-century towns, including Jacksonville, Illinois; Grass Valley, California; and Seattle, Washington. Locational advantages initially recommended each of these sites, and subsequent developments made each community more attractive to prospective settlers. Even though precise comparisons among studies of nineteenth-century communities are not always possible, the Grand Junction case supports several conclusions about life in recently settled areas.

Townspeople were central, of course, in the development of Grand Junction, as they were in other communities; but focusing solely on their actions ignores the role played by the community's economic and social attributes in attracting potential settlers and in impeding out-migration.[2] Widening the focus to include the community's character is particularly useful in understanding an evolving community like Grand Junction, where there were numerous economic, political, and social possibilities as well as uncertainty about the community's prospects for success.

The pioneer settlement of Grand Junction was distinctive from the small town that succeeded it. During the initial stage of settlement, it provided many economic opportunities. The need for such fundamental business enterprises as grocery and hardware stores and saloons was evident, and these flourished as the town's population increased. The demand for shelter was substantial; settlers required housing, and carpenters and brick masons found ready employment. Railroad construction also created jobs, particularly in road building. Many early settlers in Grand Junction were employed in such personal service occupations as cook, laundress, and waiter; in a community made up primarily of single men, a number of whom were railroad laborers, there was great demand for these services. A considerably larger proportion of men owned and operated their own businesses in the pioneer settlement than they would in the small town. Moreover, because the price of land was so low in pioneer Grand Junction anyone who wanted to could purchase property. Although the controversy between the town company and William Keith placed a "cloud" upon land titles, about half of the 1885 families had acquired town property. Outsiders obviously believed that property in the pioneer settlement held financial promise because 122 nonresidents purchased lots and paid taxes in 1885 to the Mesa County assessor.

The creation of a town where none had existed before required participation both in building political institutions and in structuring social organizations. Colorado statutes outlined the steps necessary to establish a local government: pioneers had to incorporate the town and elect aldermen. In Grand Junction, they were prodded and encouraged by the Grand Junction Town Company. When town company president George A. Crawford later succeeded in having Grand Junction named as county seat for Mesa County, pioneers celebrated the occasion. In forming the town government, settlers confronted a myriad of political problems, including the licensing of saloons, peddlers, and dogs. Pioneers also established a school district and elected board members. Solving these problems associated with town formation elicited a high degree of citizen participation and resulted in large voter turnout at elections.

Although they surrendered certain aspects of community building to the town company, settlers readily instituted churches and voluntary associations. Concerned about protection, they established (in 1882) a local militia and a volunteer fire department. They also initiated social organizations, and by 1885 fourteen such groups were established in the community. Included among these organizations were the Pioneer and Historical Society, the GAR, and the Board of Trade. Women, whose focus was directed toward home and child-rearing, participated less frequently than men, although they did form a chapter of the WCTU, which lasted for more than two decades.

As the climate of uncertainty passed and Grand Junction's identity as a small town emerged, day-to-day life changed. In the pioneer settlement, such enterprises as grocery and hardware stores met the needs of settlers; but by the early 1890s there was a demand for specialty stores. At the same time, the statistical evidence points to a slight decline in the number of independent businessmen in the commercial setting, as several national and regional companies opened branches in the community and employed local residents.[3] Occupational opportunity in Grand Junction remained undiminished, particularly for artisans and men involved in transportation and communication. By 1900 the occupational structure was both more diverse and more specialized. More than half of those employed reported skilled occupations. For example, the proportion of the population that worked for the railroad increased over this period. The nature of the jobs changed as well. At first, laborers had been in demand as track was laid between Pueblo and Salt Lake City and depots erected; once that construction was finished, operators (engineers, brakemen, and conductors) and maintenance personnel replaced the laborers. At the same time, the proportion of the population employed in personal services declined as railroad laborers moved on and as personal service tasks were absorbed by the families that took in boarders.[4]

As a small town, Grand Junction continued to provide occasions for political and social activities. Obtaining safe and adequate water was the cardinal issue confronting the community in the 1890s, but other problems also attracted attention. Prohibition stimulated some political activity, as did the question of free silver. As a result, voter turnout at elections remained high. Not only did citizens turn out to voice their opinions about drinking water and drinking alcohol; they also decided who would be mayor and who would sit on the town's council. Settlers believed that these responsibilities should be shared. Between 1882, when Charles Shanks was elected as the first mayor, and 1901, when Wendell P. Ela was named to his third term, thirteen men held that position. The forty-five men elected to the town's council in the first two decades were drawn from all walks of life, and few served a second term.[5]

Voluntary associations multiplied as Grand Junction matured, enabling settlers to participate in a wide range of organizations. Turn-of-the-century Grand Junction had at least thirty-eight formal voluntary associations, and about one in every three families belonged to some organization. While these figures also demonstrate that most residents in small-town families were not members of any association, the level of participation was more than double of that found in the longer-settled cities.[6] The types of associations changed over time. Once they were no longer worried about Indian attacks, townspeople disbanded the militia. On the other hand, fire protection remained a topic of paramount concern, and residents willingly paid a permanent force of fire fighters. Fraternal organizations with national affiliations claimed large memberships, particularly as these groups initiated female auxiliaries. Other clubs also provided opportunities for women to participate in community building, and in 1900 the community had more than a dozen women's groups. The completion of the public library attests to the success of women's organizations.

The data from Grand Junction, as well as from other community studies, support the stereotypical picture of life in small towns—a picture that, to a great extent, has been shaped by fiction and autobiography. In his 1954 depiction of small-town life, historian Lewis Atherton drew on these sources as well as newspapers. According to Atherton, the typical midwestern town had a simple economy made up of general stores, barbershops, saloons, drugstores, hotels, and mills; businesses that were all locally controlled. Artisans prospered in the relatively isolated and noncomplex setting. Atherton overlooked the issues and candidates of local politics, focusing instead on political activity during presidential contests. Residents of small towns were "joiners," Atherton claimed, and they preferred organizations that were open to everyone. Everyone knew everyone in the small town; they even "knew the color and shape of every home in town," a town in which the family was the dominant social unit.[7]

In many aspects, this image of economic, political, and social life in the small town during the middle to late nineteenth century is accurate—whether it is Grand Junction, Jacksonville, early Seattle, Grass Valley, or towns in Trempealeau County. The commercial community did have a variety of enterprises, most of them locally owned and unspecialized. The small town did provide a wide selection of employment. Once a community had access to a railroad, however, outside businesses moved in, bringing with them specialization both in commercial enterprises and in the labor market. The small town did accommodate political activity, although more often than not it was conflict that encouraged participation. Moreover, citizens frequently paid greater attention to local issues than to national ones. Small towns like Grand Junction were communities where it was possible for everyone to know nearly everyone else.[8]

The comparison of life in a pioneer community with that in a small town raises questions about the transitions between the two. One aim of this study has been to identify these indices of transition that could signify when the tentative settlement—the pioneer settlement—had become a small town that seemed assured of continued existence. The Grand Junction case suggests several arenas in which such evolution may be measured: demographic, economic, and participative. Increased community consciousness also provides an index of transition.

The sweeping demographic changes experienced by Grand Junction furnish one measure of transition. The pioneer settlement had been characterized by a preponderance of males in their early thirties who were single and lived alone, a trait that Grand Junction shared with Kansas cattle towns and California mining towns. In the small town of 1900, there were as many women as men, and most adults were wed. The small town also had a more balanced age distribution: there were many children and old people. Moreover, almost everyone, regardless of marital status, resided in private homes, if not as owners or renters then as boarders.[9]

Grand Junction's changed business environment and its modified occupational structure also suggest indices of transition. Independently owned stores, which sold groceries, hardware, and liquor, were characteristic of the pioneer settlement. More highly specialized enterprises, on the other hand, were unstable during the first few years and seldom endured. The decline in the number of independent owners and the increase is managers and agents representing outside companies marked Grand Junction's transition to a small town. At the same time, specialty stores were increasingly more successful. Grand Junction's occupational structure experienced similar transitions. In the pioneer settlement, most workers provided food and shelter; in the small town, the labor force was both more diverse and specialized. The increased percentage of skilled workers in turn-of-the-century Grand Junction suggests that in new towns of the late nineteenth century, particularly those that were railroad service centers, finding employment was not difficult.

Significantly increased participation by women offers a third measure of transition. In Grand Junction's pioneer period, very few women participated in the two associations open to them; but with the emergence of the small town, women became much more active in the community. This increased participation of women in Grand Junction's voluntary community reflects several changes. First, there were many more women in the community by the late 1890s, as reflected in the sex ratio. Second, the number of female associations had multiplied, particularly auxiliaries to fraternal organizations and women's clubs. In Colorado, the woman suffrage movement also sparked participation. Initially, women worked to gain passage of the amendment, and then they moved into politics. Third, the aging of the adult population, which occurred as Grand Junction's pioneer period passed, also influenced women's participation. As their child-rearing and other domestic duties decreased, women could look to activities beyond their homes.[10]

As a result of the controversy concerning water, Grand Junction matured politically and developed a community consciousness. That maturation provides another measure of transition. More than any other facet of community building, the water issue exposes the stages of the evolution from pioneer settlement to a small town. What began as a desire on the part of settlers for fire protection and reliable domestic water supply developed over subsequent years into a vehicle for local control. Dissatisfaction first with the Grand Junction Town Company and then with an outside corporation evolved into a determination on the part of residents to control the utility themselves. Three phases marked this process. The first phase dated from the town's incorporation in June 1882, and was characterized by a willingness on the part of the citizens to allow the Grand Junction Town Company to provide water. An intermediate stage commenced in July 1888, when residents granted a franchise to an outside firm. Although they were convinced of their dissatisfaction with the town company, they were hesitant about the risks surrounding municipal ownership. However, problems with the franchise company over the following years convinced more and more residents that municipal ownership was the best solution. When they voted in December 1894 to assume that responsibility, they also took a major step forward in community self-consciousness. In other communities, such events as reform or economic boom provided the catalyst for

CONCLUSION

self-consciousness. The issue, however, was much less important than the community cohesiveness that resulted.[11]

Mediating all these transitions was the family, and indeed, the family itself furnishes an index of change. Family formation among settlers, coupled with the settlement of additional families, thoroughly altered living arrangements in Grand Junction as the community matured. In 1885 more than half of the town's population resided in "no-family" households of some sort; in 1900 fewer than one-fifth lived in such residential situations. Family composition also provides evidence of metamorphosis. The proportion of families with children almost doubled, and the number of families including boarders or lodgers increased by a factor of three. The increase in the number of families in the community helps to explain this boarding phenomenon. In 1885 there simply were few families with whom to board, and the only option available was the large boardinghouse or hotel. By 1900 another alternative was present, and boarders and lodgers opted for the private homes of families rather than hotels as living quarters.[12]

The family's influence in mediating the transitions from pioneer settlement to small town extended beyond the immediate family to include a kinship network. Even during the initial stages of community building in Grand Junction, when there was an abundance of single men, kinship played an important role in migration and settlement. Then, one in every five families belonged to a kinship network that extended beyond the simple family. Whether in western Colorado or on the Overland Trail to Oregon and Washington, pioneers often migrated with in-laws as well as blood relatives.[13] As the community matured, the kinship network became broader and more complex—partly as a result of marriages and partly because of the continued settlement of families. By the turn of the century, about one-third of the community had other relatives in the town.[14]

Grand Junction experienced a great deal of change during the 1880s and 1890s, yet many of the problems that often promote population turnover were missing. Economic opportunity in terms of occupation and property was available; participation remained open in political decision making; and the number and range of voluntary associations demonstrated that a variety of social options existed. Nevertheless, Grand Junction did not seem particularly successful in holding its pioneer population. Only about one-quarter of the families counted in 1885 remained fifteen years later.

Population turnover has often been cited as an impediment to the building of frontier communities, and it would be easy to conclude that Grand Junction's high population turnover meant that the community was unsuccessful. Robert V. Hine, for instance, has argued that "mobility, because it generated strong individualism and weak social intimacy, nullified community." To some observers, the constant ebb and flow of people might indicate instability, for if Grand Junction, or any community, could not retain its residents, how could it possibly prosper?[15]

In light of the findings about Grand Junction, perhaps population turnover should be looked at differently. Like Grass Valley, Nevada City, Seattle, and other communities that survived, and in some cases thrived, Grand Junction continued to grow despite high rates of emigration. Although such migration exhibited the volatility of the frontier, at the same time it performed several social functions in a town. One of these functions was to drain the town of dissidents and others who "didn't fit in." Several scholars have suggested that the ambivalence between the community ideal and individual freedom help in explaining emigration. As one points out,

> When the community demanded too high a price in the freedom of an individual—whether demanding that a man be content with his economic lot or that he adhere to doctrines of the ruling church, say—he broke the ties and moved off alone or with a like-minded group of others, seeking to found a better community.[16]

Among these individuals were writers like Sinclair Lewis, but thousands of others, less well known, also moved away from towns where they were dissatisfied. To be sure, pressures on individuals and families to fit in or move on grew tremendous as they tried to find places to settle, but for the community that emigration alleviated much potential strife.

Emigration also meant, as study after study shows, that those who stayed were more likely to be elected to public office, become wealthier, and actively participate in voluntary associations.[17] This population turnover was particularly important to "young, untried men," Ralph Mann concludes, because it gave them "a chance to exercise authority and to take important places in town economic life." Involvement in the town's economy, politics, and associative activities, in conjunction with kin relationships, resulted in the "binding ties

CONCLUSION 115

[and] commonly assumed values" that underlie a community. That involvement also provided those who stayed with a strong voice in determining the form of their community.[18]

While community change has been the focus of this study, it is critical to recognize that individual people experienced such changes: people like James Bucklin, Emma Kent, Edwin and Lulu Price, Charles and Nellie McCarey, and J. H. and Ella Belle Ackerman and their children. In Grand Junction's early years, the people who were involved in incipient community building were single males; by 1900 (and probably sooner) they were members of families. This transition from a community of single people to one comprised of families permeated all aspects of community life.

Precisely when Grand Junction's continuance was assured is difficult to discern; but by the mid-1890s, unlike the inhabitants of so many other frontier communities, Grand Junction settlers no longer seemed to worry that their town might fail. They had successfully addressed many of the economic, political, and social problems that confronted frontier towns, and their community had evolved into a confident small town. However, Grand Junction's maturation was far from complete. Over the subsequent years, the community confronted critical issues associated with its economy, successfully campaigning for Colorado's first sugar beet factory. Municipal reform remained in the political forefront, and in 1909 Grand Junction adopted charter revisions that drew nationwide attention as a model of town government. Grand Junction's residents instinctively knew that town building was a dynamic process, and as they worked to establish and to maintain the community's position as the central town of Colorado's western slope, they also ensured its continuance.

APPENDIX 1
Social Network Analysis

To understand social relationships, I utilized social network analysis, a technique designed by social anthropologists and most frequently used to understand how husbands and wives adapt to changing environments. Researchers interview families asking about genealogy, courtship, childrearing, occupation, housing, and activities not specifically related to the home. The methodology is helpful because it suggests a conceptual framework for the variety of interactions among individuals and groups, and it furnishes a useful way of reconstructing social relationships in Grand Junction. (See Elizabeth Bott, *Family and Social Network: Roles, Norms, and External Relationships in Ordinary Urban Families*, 2d ed. [New York, 1971]; "General Introduction" in Charles Tilly, ed., *An Urban World* [Boston, 1974]; Thomas Bender, *Community and Social Change in America;* (New Brunswick, N.J., 1978), 121–28, esp.; and Darrett Rutman, "Community Study," *Historical Methods* 13 [1980]:29–41.)

While it was clearly impossible to interview the settlers of Grand Junction, I created an "interview form" that asked many of the same questions asked by contemporary researchers. Then, I "answered" the questions with the available data. Often, I could answer questions about genealogy, courtship (if a marriage resulted), occupation, and activities outside the home. In this manner, I was able to perceive kin relationships more clearly. In addition, responses to questions about activities outside the home led to an understanding of the affiliate network.

I was especially interested in women's experience. After 1880, the census provided a great deal of information for understanding women's kinship. When a woman told the census enumerator that she was the head of household's mother-in-law or sister-in-law, it was evident that the wife had kin nearby. When kin did not share a dwelling, tracing women's relationships became problematic but not impossible. Marriage records were a second source for studying women, and I used them in two ways. First, I searched the Mesa County marriage records for all girls who were listed in the 1885 census, to see if they had wed and who they had married, and thereby established their relationships. Second, because the 1900 census noted how long a couple had been married I checked the marriage records for those who had been wed for less than fifteen years. This search uncovered many women's maiden names. I was then able to tie married women to their families of origin and to establish kin relationships. For families who settled in Grand Junction after 1885, this second procedure was particularly useful. The newspapers sometimes provided information about local people who had married elsewhere.

I also used the "interview form" to explain relationships or networks beyond the family. Certainly, I can draw no firm conclusions about the intensity of such networks—how friendly the people were, for example—but I can demonstrate the possibility and likelihood of social interaction. The "cohesiveness" of the affiliate network was measured by the use of a matrix. Subjects—in this case, families—are listed along the edges of the matrix in the same order (usually at the top and left margins), and the connections between subjects are

	Marsh	Cameron	Nichols	Russell	Lumsden	Bucklin	Crawford	Miller
Marsh	–	1	0	1	2	0	0	1
Cameron	1	–	0	1	0	0	0	1
Nichols	0	0	–	2	1	1	1	1
Russell	1	1	2	–	0	2	1	2
Lumsden	2	0	1	0	–	1	0	0
Bucklin	0	0	1	2	1	–	1	2
Crawford	0	0	1	1	0	1	–	2
Miller	1	1	1	2	0	2	2	–

FIGURE 6: Matrix of Social Connections

entered into the matrix as Figure 6 shows. W. A. Marsh, for example, was connected through his memberships to J. M. Cameron, O. D. Russell, and A. A. Miller. Marsh and J. J. Lumsden shared two organizations. Once all of the connections between families have been noted, a measure of cohesiveness may be derived by "dividing the total number of mutual choices ($\Sigma[i \leftrightarrow j]$) by the number of possible pairs ($n[n-1]/2$)." The more cohesive a community is, the larger the quotient will be. The matrix for Grand Junction's pioneer period was 113×113 and for the more stable period 292×292. The cohesiveness measure for the pioneer period was .246 and for the stable town, .173. (See H. W. Smith, *Strategies of Social Research*, 2d ed. [Englewood Cliffs, N.J., 1981], 316–17. A more complete discussion may be found in Gardner Lindzey and Donn Byrne, "Measurement of Social Change and Interpersonal Attractiveness," in Gardner Lindzey and Elliot Aronson, eds., *The Handbook of Social Psychology*, 2d ed. [Reading, Mass., 1966], 445–56, 463–67.)

APPENDIX 2
Estimates of Voter Eligibility

Because participation as measured by election turnout is central to my study, I needed some idea of how many people were eligible to vote in any single election. Except for elections approving municipal indebtedness, Colorado law specified that every male over the age of twenty-one who was a citizen or intending to become a U.S. citizen was entitled to vote in all elections, providing that he met residency requirements. Only taxpayers could vote in elections that put the municipality in debt. (See *General Statutes of the State of Colorado, 1883* [Denver, 1883], chap. XXXIV, par. 1150; chap. CIX, pars. 3419–3424 [pars. 3419 and 3423, esp.].) A law requiring formal registration was enacted in 1891, but the registration books were not preserved. (See *Laws Passed at the Ninth Session of the General Assembly of the State of Colorado, 1893* [Denver, 1893], S.B. 410, pp. 244–55.) Therefore, I estimated voter eligibility—both for ordinary elections and for those involving municipal debt—by utilizing data that were available to me. I undertook two analyses: one to estimate the number of voters eligible to vote in municipal, general, and county elections; the other to assess the number of voters eligible to vote in elections that placed the community in debt.

Two sources provided data for estimating the number of settlers who could vote in regular elections. One was the population in the censuses from 1885 to 1920. I diagrammed those figures (859; 2,030; 3,503; 7,754; and 8,665, respectively) and then connected the points in a curvilinear fashion. Figure 7 shows estimated population in-

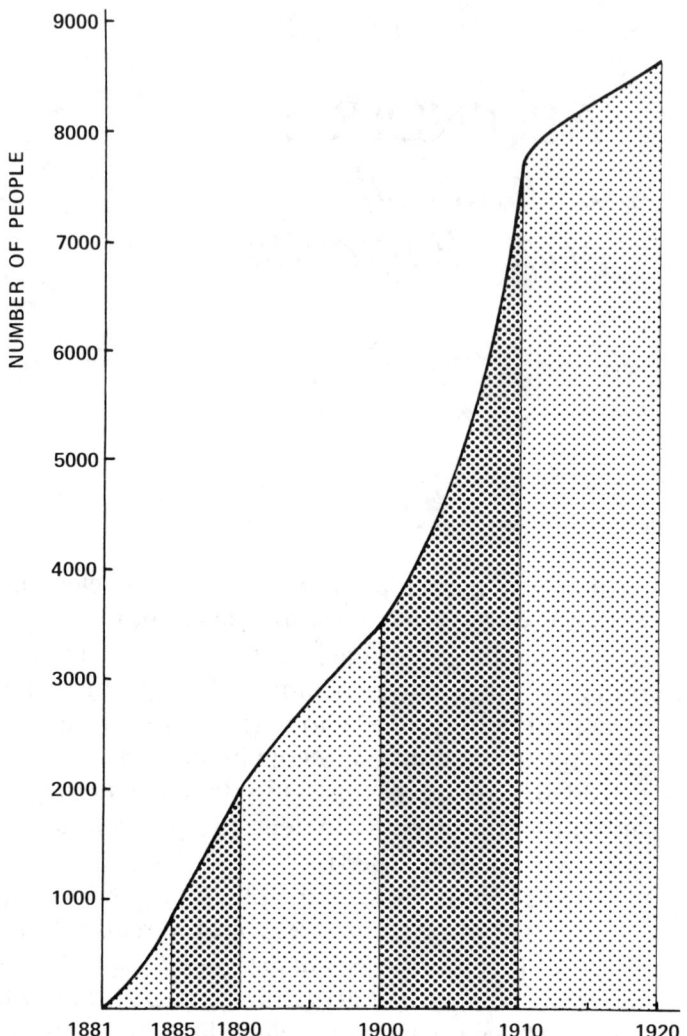

FIGURE 7: Estimated Population Increase, 1881 to 1920

crease. The other source that I used to estimate eligibility was the random sample of males and females drawn from the manuscripts of the 1885 and 1900 censuses. In 1885 males eligible to vote made up 43.4 percent of the population; by 1900 that percentage had declined to 32.5 percent, in large part because there were more children in the town. The proportion of females of voting age in-

ESTIMATES OF VOTER ELIGIBILITY 123

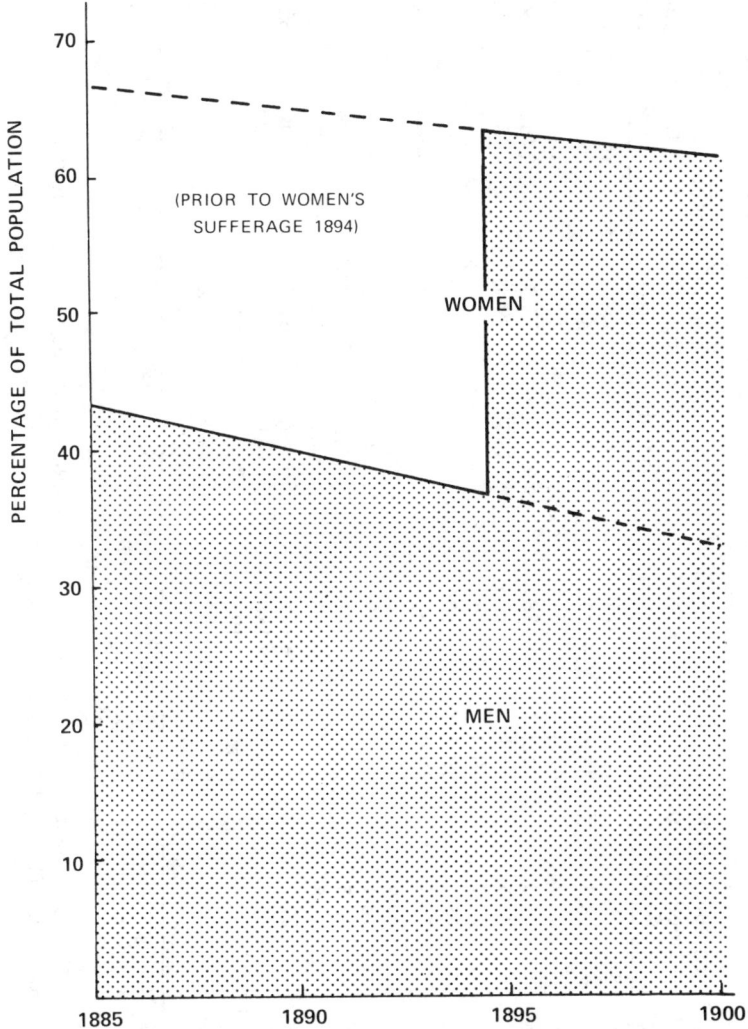

FIGURE 8: Percentage Eligible to Vote in Regular Elections

creased slightly over the period—from 23.3 percent to 28.5 percent—again, a result of the stabilization of the population. Figure 8 displays in these two enumerations the percentage of males and females aged twenty-one years and older, and points out the change in eligible voters over fifteen years. The solid line shows how woman suffrage increased the pool of eligible voters.

Table 11
Estimated Eligible Voters at Municipal, General, and County Elections Compared to Actual Turnout

year	estimated[a] population (1)	Percent Eligible Voters (population aged 20+)[b] male (2)	Percent Eligible Voters (population aged 20+)[b] female (3)	Percent Eligible Voters (population aged 20+)[b] total[c] (4)	estimated number[e] eligible voters[d] (5)	Turnout Municipal actual[e] (6)	Turnout Municipal percent[f] (7)	Turnout General/County actual[g] (8)	Turnout General/County percent[h] (9)
1885	859*	43.3	23.3	43.3	372	255	68.5		
1886	1200	42.6	23.7	42.6	511				
1887	1400	41.9	24.0	41.9	587			348	59.3
1888	1600	41.1	24.5	41.1	656	193	29.4		
1889	1820	40.4	24.7	40.4	735			488	74.4
1890	2030*	39.7	25.1	39.7	806				
1891	2120	39.0	25.4	39.0	827	574	69.4		
1892	2270	38.3	25.8	38.3	869			491	56.6
1893	2390	37.5	26.1	37.5	896	483	53.9	430	53.7
1894	2400	36.8	26.5	63.3	1519	740	48.7	925	60.9
1895	2680	36.1	26.8	62.9	1686	987	58.5	1037	61.5
1896	2810	35.4	27.2	62.6	1759	1087	61.8	1090	62.0
1897	3000	34.7	27.5	62.2	1866	861	46.1	811	43.5
1898	3180	33.9	27.9	61.8	1925	1022	52.0	844	43.0
1899	3310	33.2	28.2	61.4	2032	1040	51.2		
1900	3503*	32.5	28.5	61.0	2137	1210	56.6		

* Actual, not estimated, number.
[a] See Figure 7.
[b] See Figure 8.
[c] Until 1894 women could not vote in Colorado; therefore, the percentage old enough to vote is not included until that date.
[d] Derived by multiplying Estimated Population (1) and % Eligible Voters (4).
[e] As reported in the newspapers.
[f] Actual Turnout (6) divided by Estimated Number Eligible Voters (5).
[g] As reported in the newspapers. General elections were held in even-numbered years and county elections in odd-numbered years.
[h] Actual Turnout (8) divided by Estimated Number Eligible Voters (5).

To find the number of eligible voters in any specific year, I multiplied estimated population by the percentage eligible to vote. Table 11 exhibits the results of such calculations and provides comparisons with actual turnout. (Merle Curti was also interested in the number of eligible voters. To project eligibility, he relied on census data at five-year intervals. See Curti, *The Making of an American Community, A Case Study of Democracy in a Frontier County* [Stanford, 1959]: 335–37.)

I followed the same technique in estimating the number of persons who could place the town in debt. Again, two sources provided the necessary data. One was the tax assessments, which listed everyone who held either real or personal property; the other was the manuscripts of the 1885 and 1900 censuses, which identified Grand Junction's resident population. (See Chapter 2.) In 1885, 176 men and 39 women paid taxes in Grand Junction (in an adult population of 406 men and 197 women); in 1900, 262 men and 135 women were taxpayers (among 1,215 men and 993 women). Figure 9 presents the changes in property holding. Again, the solid line shows the impact of woman suffrage. Table 12 indicates the elections in which town residents voted on municipal indebtedness. To determine the percentage of turnout, I compared actual turnout to estimated eligibility.

The assumption underlying these tabulations are, at best, problematic. First, I have assumed that population change—whether in the aggregate figures of the printed census or as derived in the random sample—occurred at the same rate each year. Because it ignores the effect of such economic change as the depression in the early 1890s, such an assumption is ahistorical; nevertheless, no information is available that might better predict interim change.

Second, I have presumed that everyone old enough to vote and/or everyone holding property also met the residency requirements. The effect of this assumption is an overestimation of voter eligibility, and possibly, an underestimation in the percentage of turnout.

The third assumption relates to determining exactly who was eligible to vote in indebtedness elections. In particular, if a married couple held property in one spouse's name only, were both eligible to vote or just the property holder? Colorado law declared:

> The treasurer of the county ... shall make out ... a certified list of the taxpayers of such city or town, who shall have paid taxes upon property assessed to them, in

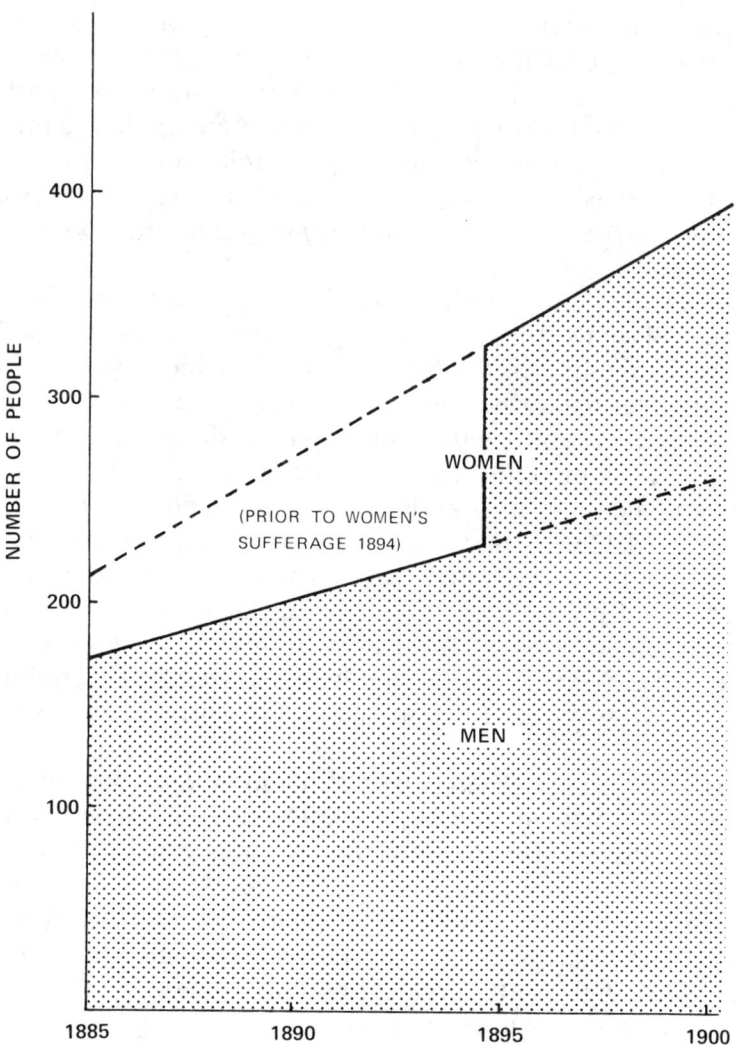

FIGURE 9: Population Eligible to Vote in Indebtedness Elections

Table 12
Estimated Eligible Voters in Elections Incurring Municipal Debts

year	Estimated Eligible Voters			Turnout	
	male[a]	female[a]	total[b]	actual[c]	percent[d]
1885	176*	39*	176	—	—
1894	227	97	324	284	87.7
1897	244	116	360	229	63.6
1898	250	122	372	328	88.1
1899	256	129	385	332	86.2
1900	262*	135*	397	—	—

*Persons enumerated in either the 1885 or 1900 census who owned property.
[a] See Figure 9.
[b] Until 1894 women could not vote in Colorado; therefore property-holding women are excluded until then.
[c] As reported in the newspapers.
[d] Actual Turnout divided by Estimated Eligible Voters.

the preceding year, and no person shall vote upon the question of funding the city or town indebtedness unless his name shall appear upon such certified list.... (*General Statutes of the State of Colorado, 1883,* chap. CIX, par. 3419).

I have assumed that election officials followed the letter of the law and permitted only those persons who were listed as property holders to vote. If property was held in the husband's name alone, his wife was not counted as an eligible voter; similarly, in cases where the wife was named as taxpayer, the husband was not tallied.

APPENDIX 3
Voluntary Associations

The newspapers were not always clear about the exact date an organization was started; thus, some of the following dates may be incorrect by a year or two.

1882   Methodist Episcopal Church South
             Company F, Grand Valley Guards

1883   Volunteer Fire Department
             GAR
             WCTU
             Masons, Mesa Lodge, No. 55
             Baptist Church
             Methodist Episcopal Church
             Presbyterian Church

1884   Grand Junction Board of Trade
             Chautauqua Literary and Scientific Circle
             Mesa County Fair Association
             Mesa County Horticultural Society
             IOOF, Mesa Lodge, No. 58
             Western Colorado Stock Grower's Association
             Knights of Honor
             Christian Church
             Catholic Church

APPENDIX THREE

1885   Library Association
Pioneer and Historical Society

1886   Amateur Dramatic Club
German Club
Industrial Club
Jockey Club
Knights of Labor, No. 3524
International Brotherhood of Locomotive Engineers, No. 488
Women's Relief Corps
Independent Order of Good Templars

1887   Social Literary Society

1888   Grand Junction Club

1889   Rifle Club

1890   Congregational Church
Episcopal Church

1891   Amazon Guards
Knights of Pythias
Patriotic Sons of America
Phoenix Social Club
Silver Crescent Band
Terpsicorean Society
International Brotherhood of Railway Trainmen
Western Colorado Congress
Woodmen of the World
Royal Arch Masons

1892   Western Colorado Academy of Science
Queen Isabella Study Club
Mandolin Club
Grand Junction Wheel Club
YMCA
African Methodist Episcopal Church

1893   Ancient Order of United Workmen
        Children's Home Society
        Keeley Institute
        Knights Templar
        Turn Verein
        Woman's Suffrage League
        Christian Science Church

1894   Glee Club
        Peach Day
        Political Science Club
        Ralston Health Club
        Swimming Club

1895   Grand Junction Athletic Association
        Real Estate Exchange
        Daughters of Rebekah
        Rathbone Sisters
        Typographical Union
        Twentieth-Century Woman's Club

1896   Camera Club
        Order of Select Friends
        Shakespeare Club
        Grand Mesa Woman's Club

1897   Sons of Civil War Veterans
        Order of Railway Conductors, No. 325

1898   Daughters of Pocahontas
        Improved Order of Redmen
        Women of Woodcraft
        Mesa County Teachers Association

1899   no data

1900   Pioneers of the Pacific
        Young Men's Cultural Club
        Art League

NOTES

Introduction

1. Henry S. Canby, *The Age of Confidence* (New York, 1934), 1.
2. *Time*, 24 May 1976, 16.
3. Growing up in a small town has been a central feature of many autobiographies, including those by Susan Allen Toth, *Blooming: A Small Town Girlhood* (New York, 1978); Bruce Catton, *Waiting for the Morning Train: An American Boyhood* (New York, 1972); and Walter O'Meara, *We Made It Through the Winter: A Memoir of a Northern Minnesota Boyhood* (Minneapolis, 1974). Richard Lingeman's *Small Town America: A Narrative History, 1620-the Present* (New York, 1980) provides a narrative examination of small-town life from Puritan settlement to the present day, as portrayed by American writers. Well-known examples include: Sherwood Anderson, *Winesburg, Ohio* (New York, 1919); Willa Cather, *Song of the Lark* (New York, 1915); Sarah Orne Jewett, *The Country of the Pointed Firs* (New York, 1896); Sinclair Lewis, *Main Street* (New York, 1921); Edgar Lee Masters, *Spoon River Anthology* (New York, 1915); Booth Tarkington, *The Gentleman From Indiana* (New York, 1899); Mark Twain, *The Man That Corrupted Hadleyburg* (New York, 1900); Thornton Wilder, *Our Town: A Play in Three Acts* (New York, 1938). A photographic essay of small-town life during the last quarter of the nineteenth century and the first quarter of the twentieth is found in Stephen W. Sears, *Hometown U.S.A.* (New York, 1975).
4. Lingeman, *Small Town America*, chaps. 6–8, passim; and Anthony Channel Hilfer, *The Revolt from the Village, 1915–1930* (Chapel Hill, 1969).
5. Helen Hooven Santmyer, *". . . And Ladies of the Club"* (Columbus, Ohio, 1982); Garrison Keillor, *Lake Wobegon Days* (New York, 1985).

6. Partly out of concern over the decline of rural population, sociologists began studying such places in the early twentieth century. An early example is Wilbert L. Anderson, *The Country Town: A Study of Rural Evolution* (New York, 1906); other examples include Albert Blumenthal, *A Sociological Study of a Small Town* (Chicago, 1932), Granville Hicks, *Small Town* (New York, 1946); and more recently, Arthur J. Vidich and Joseph Bensman, *Small Town in Mass Society: Class, Power, and Religion in a Rural Community*, rev. ed., (Princeton, 1968). The journal *Rural Sociology* is devoted to research in this arena. Geographers and economists have studied functions provided by towns; for example, Howard A. J. Stafford, "The Functional Bases of Small Towns," *Economic Geography* 39 (1963); and James B. Kenyou, "On the Relation Between Central Functions and Size of Place," *Annals of the Association of American Geographers* 57 (1967). Community power has been a major focus for such political scientists as Aaron Widavsky, *Leadership in a Small Town* (Totowa, N.J., 1964); and Everett Carll Ladd, *Ideology in America* (Ithaca, 1960), 186–223, esp.

7. A list of studies examining towns in the colonial and early national periods would include Hal S. Barron, *Those Who Stayed Behind: Rural Society in Nineteenth-Century New England* (Cambridge, 1984); Carl Bridenbaugh, *Cities in the Wilderness: The First Century of Urban Life in America, 1625–1742* (New York, 1938) and *Cities in Revolt: Urban Life in America, 1743–1776* (New York, 1955); John Demos, *A Little Commonwealth: Family Life in Plymouth Colony* (New York, 1970); Charles S. Grant, *Democracy in the Connecticut Frontier Town of Kent* (New York, 1961); Philip J. Greven, Jr., *Four Generations: Population, Land, and Family in Colonial Andover, Massachusetts* (Ithaca, 1970); Kenneth Lockridge, *A New England Town: The First Hundred Years* (New York, 1969); Sumner Chilton Powell, *Puritan Village: The Formation of a New England Town* (Middleton, Conn., 1963); Darrett B. Rutman, *Winthrop's Boston: Portrait of a Puritan Town, 1630–1649* (Chapel Hill, 1965) and *Husbandmen of Plymouth: Farms and Villages in the Old Colony, 1620–1692* (Boston, 1967); Richard C. Wade, *The Urban Frontier: The Rise of Cities, 1790–1830* (Cambridge, Mass., 1959); John J. Waters, "Hingham, Massachusetts, 1631–1661; An East Anglican Oligarchy in the New World," *Journal of Social History* 1(1967–1968); and Michael Zuckerman, *Peaceable Kingdoms: New England Towns in the Eighteenth Century* (New York, 1970).

8. In his recent study of Chelsea, Vermont; Barron also calls attention to the shadows that industrialization and urbanization have cast on the study of nonurban life. See Barron, *Those Who Stayed Behind*, xi, 1. Generally, the small towns that have merited study in the middle and late nineteenth century have been those on the frontier: Robert R. Dykstra, *The Cattle Towns* (New York, 1968); William G. Robbins, "Opportunity and Persistence in the Pacific Northwest: A Quantitative Study of Early Roseburg, Oregon," *Pacific Historical Review* 39 (1970); Ralph Mann, *After the Gold Rush: Society in Grass Valley and Nevada City, California, 1849–1870* (Stanford, 1982); Richard S. Alcorn, "Leadership and Stability in Mid-Nineteenth-Century America:

A Case Study," *Journal of American History* 61 (1974); Gilbert Stelter, "The City and Westward Expansion: A Western Case Study," *Western Historical Quarterly* 4 (1973); Don Harrison Doyle, *The Social Order of a Frontier Community: Jacksonville, Illinois, 1825–1870* (Urbana, 1978); and John C. Hudson, *Plains Country Towns* (Minneapolis, 1985).

9. Robert H. Wiebe, *The Search for Order* (New York, 1967), 11–75, esp.; Page Smith, *As a City upon a Hill: The Town in American History* (Cambridge, Mass., 1966), 282; and George Mowry, *The Urban Nation* (New York, 1965), 1. Other historians who concur include Samuel P. Hays, *The Response to Industrialism, 1885–1914* (Chicago, 1957); and John A. Garraty, *The New Commonwealth, 1877–1890* (New York, 1968), 179–219.

10. *Historical Statistics of the United States from Colonial Times to 1970* (Washington, D.C., 1975), A57–72.

11. U.S. Bureau of the Census, *Thirteenth Census of the United States: 1910: Population*, Vol. 1 (Washington, D.C., 1913), 67. U.S. Bureau of the Census. *Nineteenth Census of the united States: 1970. Census of Population*, Vol. 1 (Washington, D.C., 1973), 72–73.

12. Two historians who have addressed the problems caused by this dichotomy are Oliver Knight, "Toward an Understanding of the Western Town," *Western Historical Quarterly*, 4 (1973); and Ronald C. Tobey, "How Urbane Was the Urbanite?" *Historical Methods Newsletter* 7 (1973–1974).

13. Geographers, for example, have developed the idea of an "urban hierarchy" as a way of ranking population concentrations according to function (see Richard L. Morrill, *The Spatial Organization of Society* [Belmont, Calif., 1966], 75–90, esp.), but there is disagreement among them about precisely how population size relates to function. An overview of how different geographers have established urban hierarchies may be found in Tobey, "How Urbane Was the Urbanite?" Rural sociologists have identified the "rural–urban continuum" in order to discuss urban processes; and George A. Hillery, Jr., surveys that continuum in "Definitions of Community: Areas of Agreement," *Rural Sociology* 20 (1955).

14. See Lewis Atherton, *Main Street on the Middle Border* (Bloomington, Ind., 1954); Dykstra, *Cattle Towns*, 2; Stelter, "The City and Westward Expansion," 189; and Doyle, *Social Order of a Frontier Community*, 16–17, 227–59.

Prologue

1. This phrase became so commonplace that it was used in advertising.

2. For an excellent summary of the conquest of the Utes, see Joseph G. Jorgensen, *The Sun Dance Religion: Power for the Powerless* (Chicago, 1972), 29–66; the quotation here is from p. 31. Other studies that examine the removal of the Utes include Wilson Rockwell, *The Utes: A Forgotten People*

(Denver, 1956); and Duane Vandenbusche and Duane A. Smith, *A Land Alone: Colorado's Western Slope* (Boulder, Colo., 1981), 75–81.

3. 46th Cong., 2d sess., H. Ex. Doc. 1, pt. 5, vol. 1. See, also, Walker D. Wyman, "A Preface to the Settlement of Grand Junction: The Uncompahgre Utes 'Goes West'," *Colorado Magazine* 10 (1933):23.

4. *The Domínguez-Escalante Journal,* trans. Fray Angelico Chavez, ed. Ted J. Warner (Provo, Utah, 1976). For a map of the Domínguez-Escalante route, see p. 121. For the description pertaining to Colorado's western slope, see entries dated August 7 to September 12; esp. September 1–7, pp. 10–42.

5. *Scenes in the Rocky Mountains, and in Oregon, California, New Mexico, Texas, and the Grand Prairies; . . .* [by Rufus Sage] (Philadelphia, 1846), 178–79. Joseph J. Hill provides a more detailed view in "Antoine Roubidoux, Kingpin in the Colorado River Fur Trade, 1824–1844," *Colorado Magazine* 7 (1930).

6. Gwinn Harris Heap, *Central Route to the Pacific* (Glendale, Calif., 1957), 203–9 esp.; S. N. Carvalho, *Incidents of Travel and Adventure in the Far West* (New York, 1860), 158–68, esp.; and "Report of a Route for the Pacific Railroad," 33d Cong., 1st sess., H. Ex. Doc. 129, pt. 2.

7. Until 1921, the Colorado River was called the Grand in Colorado; moreover, among many nineteenth-century explorers' reports there was also confusion about the Grand and Gunnison rivers.

8. R. B. Marcy, *Thirty Years of Army Life on the Border* (New York, 1866), 224–29. William Wing Loring, "Colonel Loring's Expedition across Colorado in 1858," *Colorado Magazine* 23 (1946); pp. 60–69 pertain to the western slope.

9. Quotation in William H. Goetzmann, *Exploration and Empire: The Explorer and the Scientist in the Winning of the West* (New York, 1966), 516.

10. William Henry Jackson, *Time Exposure* (New York, 1940). According to historian William H. Goetzmann, "Jackson's photography . . . helped create a new world for millions of Americans." See *Exploration and Empire,* 528.

11. Charles J. Kappler, comp. and ed., *Indian Affairs: Laws and Treaties,* vol. 1 (Washington, D.C., 1904, 180–86.

12. Indian Agent W. H. Berry reported the dissatisfaction of the Uncompahgre Utes in 47th Cong., 1st sess., H. Ex. Doc. 1, pt. 5, vol. 2. The Utes' unhappiness was well known, and even mentioned in Charles W. Haskell, ed., *History and Business Directory of Mesa County, Colorado,* (Grand Junction, 1886), 3.

13. Even if sold, the price for reservation lands was only $1.25 per acre—"a very low figure," Robert G. Athearn has pointed out, "for irrigable lands." See Athearn, *The Coloradans* (Albuquerque, 1976), 138.

14. 47th Cong., 2d sess., H. Ex. Doc. 1, pt. 5, vol. 2.
15. Walker D. Wyman, "Staking the First Ranch at Grand Junction, Colorado," *Colorado Magazine* 11 (1934):207.

Chapter 1

1. Crawford to "Col. McMurtrie," 25 November 1881 (photocopy of original), in George A. Crawford Collection, Stephen H. Hart Library, Archives, Colorado Historical Society (Denver), (hereafter cited as Crawford Collection).
2. James W. Bucklin, "Founding of City of Grand Junction," *The Trail* 7, no. 2 (July 1914):22.
3. William E. Connelley, *A Standard History of Kansas and Kansans*, vol. 2 (Chicago, 1918), 708, 1247; *History of Kansas* (Chicago, 1883), 1072–73, 829–30; Walker D. Wyman, "Staking the First Ranch at Grand Junction, Colorado," *Colorado Magazine* 11 (1934):206–7; *Grand Junction News*, 31 January 1891, p. 4 (hereafter cited as *News*); *Grand Junction Daily Star*, 29 January 1891, p. 1 (hereafter cited as *Daily Star*).
4. George A. Crawford Diary, 6 July 1881, Crawford Collection. Crawford wrote to his sister, on the company's stationary (Warner's position was listed on the stationary masthead), that "Al[lison] White . . . wished me to come and report on their property." (Later, White became a key investor in the Grand Junction Town Company.) George A. Crawford to "Jodie" (Josephine Crawford Rich), 3 July 1881, Crawford Collection. James W. Bucklin pointed out the connection between Mobley and Crawford in his recollection of Grand Junction's "Pioneer Days," published in a special edition of the *News*, April 1896, p. 3).
5. Diary, 17 September 1881, Crawford Collection.
6. Ibid., 23 September 1881.
7. Ibid., 26 September 1881. Bucklin later asserted that Crawford never intended to go as far as the Grand Valley, but Mobley's enthusiasm caused him to change his mind. "Our party had but one objective point," Bucklin recalled, "the mouth of the Gunnison River, while Governor Crawford had in mind a general idea of locating townsites whenever and wherever practical." However, a letter from Crawford dated several years earlier disputes Bucklin's claim. In 1877, Crawford wrote to his nephew and protégé, Thomas B. Crawford, that he hoped to establish a town "at or near the junction of the Gunnison and Grand." Bucklin's memories were reported in "Founding of City of Grand Junction," and in a paper delivered in August 1908 and cataloged in C.W.A. Pioneer Interviews, Pueblo County, pamphlet 344, document 24, 1933–1934, pp. 152–65 (the quotation is

from p. 157), Stephen H. Hart Library, Colorado Historical Society (Denver). Crawford's letter to his nephew is quoted in an unpublished paper in the Terry Mangan Collection, Stephen H. Hart Library, Archives, Colorado Historical Society (Denver).

8. The description is Bucklin's, even though he was not among this party and did not view the Grand Valley for another four months (in the middle of the winter). C.W.A. Pioneer Interviews, pp. 162–63.

9. John W. Reps, *Cities of the American West* (Princeton, 1979), x.

10. Crawford's previous experience entitled him to be president of the company (a position he held until his death in 1891), and he was to be well paid for his efforts. His diary records that he was to receive "1/3 interest and $3000.00 per year and expenses." In addition, he received authorization "to begin to pay self as money comes in." Diary, 21 June 1882, Crawford Collection.

11. The first, set out in 1887 by George Crawford and David Roberts, extended Seventh Street to the south. Two years later, W. T. Carpenter platted an addition west of the town. In 1890, three additions were accepted to the town: R. D. Mobley laid out an addition immediately west of First Street; William Keith, to the east of Twelfth Street; and J. A. K. Crawford (no relation to George Crawford) and Thomas B. Crawford, also west of First Street and between the railroad and the Grand River. In 1895, Benton Canon laid out lots immediately north of this addition.

12. See photo of original plat on page 41.

13. Bucklin, C. W. A. Pioneer Interviews, pp. 162–63.

14. Edwin Price, "Recollections of Grand Junction's First Newspaper Editor," *Colorado Magazine* 30 (1953):228.

15. A variety of sources provide the data for the family reconstructions that follow: MSS 1885 (see n. 16, below); MSS 1900 (see n. 16, below); Charles W. Haskell, ed., *History and Business Directory of Mesa County, Colorado* (Grand Junction, 1886); Mesa County tax records and marriage records; local newspapers; interviews and records from the Colorado Writers Project; *Progressive Men of Western Colorado* (Denver, 1906); and obituaries.

16. I drew random samples of 25 percent (using a random numbers table) from the two available censuses: Population Schedule of the Census of the State of Colorado, 1885, National Archives Microfilm Publications, 158, roll 6, Mesa County (hereafter cited as MSS 1885); Population Schedule of the Twelfth Census of the United States, 1900, National Archives Microfilm Publications, T623, roll 127, Colorado, Mesa County (hereafter cited as MSS 1900). I examined each census independently and constructed the profiles for both the pioneer settlement and the small town. The state of Colorado conducted the 1885 census in conjunction with the U.S. Bureau of the Census. The people responsible for the 1890 census needed estimates of how many people were in rapidly growing western states so that they could assign enumerators for the more detailed federal census. The popu-

lation distribution for Grand Junction in Figure 1 was derived from the random samples; for the West and the United States, from U.S. Bureau of Census, *Tenth Census of the United States: 1880,* vol. 1 (Washington, D.C., 1883); and U.S. Bureau of the Census, *Twelfth Census of the United States: 1900,* vol. 2, pt. 2 (Washington, D.C., 1902).

17. The technique of tracing family migration by examining children's birthplaces was outlined by Barnes F. Lathrop, *Migration into East Texas, 1835–1850* (Austin, 1949), 23–33.

18. The foregoing analysis examines all households.

19. Donald J. Bogue presents excellent regional data in *The Population of the United States* (Glencoe, Ill, 1959), esp. 113–15, 162–66, 130.

20. Merle Curti's pioneering analysis of Trempealeau County—*The Making of an American Community: A Case Study of Democracy in a Frontier County* (Stanford, 1959)—begins fourteen years after initial settlement. Other studies that commence their analysis several years after first settlement include: George Blackburn and Sherman L. Ricards Jr., "A Demographic History of the West: Nueces County, Texas, 1850," *Prologue, The Journal of the National Archives* 4 (1972), a study set twenty years after Anglo settlement and decades after the Mexican period; Blackburn and Ricards, "A Demographic History of the West: Manistee County, Michigan, 1860," *Journal of American History* 57 (1970–1971), set nineteen years later; Don Harrison Doyle, *The Social Order of a Frontier Community: Jacksonville, Illinois, 1825–1870* (Urbana, 1978), twenty-five years later; Richard S. Alcorn, "Leadership and Stability in Mid-Nineteenth-Century America: A Case Study," *Journal of American History* 61 (1974), twenty-seven years later; and John Modell, "Family and Fertility on the Indiana Frontier, 1820," *American Quarterly* 23 (1971), thirty years later. There are a few demographic studies of the first years of settlement; among them: Mildred Thorne, "A Population Study of an Iowa County in 1850," *Iowa Journal of History* 57 (1959); Sherman L. Ricards, Jr., "A Demographic History of the West: Butte County, California, 1850," *Papers of the Michigan Academy of Science, Arts, and Letters* 46 (1961); and Ralph Mann, *After the Gold Rush: Society in Grass Valley and Nevada City, California, 1849–1870* (Stanford, 1982).

21. Richard C. Wade, *The Urban Frontier: The Rise of Cities, 1790–1830* (Cambridge, Mass., 1959); Gunther Barth, *Instant Cities: Urbanization and the Rise of San Francisco and Denver* (New York, 1975); Roger Lotchin, *San Francisco, 1846–1856: From Hamlet to City* (New York, 1974); Kenneth W. Wheeler, *To Wear a City's Crown: The Beginnings of Urban Growth in Texas, 1836–1865* (Cambridge, Mass., 1968); and Robert L. Martin, *The City Moves West: Economic and Industrial Growth in Central West Texas* (Austin, 1969). For a general review of the literature of the city in the West, see Bradford Luckingham, "The City in the Westward Movement—A Bibliographical Note," *Western Historical Quarterly* 5 (1974).

22. George Blackburn and Sherman L. Ricards, Jr., have calculated

median ages for several frontier locales. Except for Butte, Montana, the median age for men ranged from 20.27 to 23.85; for women, from 16.63 to 18.78. In more urbanized Butte, as in Grand Junction, the median age was much higher: 27.84 for men, and 22.60 for women. See Blackburn and Ricards, "Demographic History of the West: Manistee County," 605–6.

23. Compare the age pyramids for Robert R. Dykstra, *The Cattle Towns* (New York, 1968), 247, with those of Grand Junction.

Chapter 2

1. Crawford to David C. Dodge, 30 November 1881 (photocopy of original), Crawford Collection.

2. For a discussion of the historical development of settlements and settlement systems, see, for example, Charles F. J. Whebell, "Corridors: A Theory of Urban Systems," *Annals of the Association of American Geographers* 59 (1969); F. A. Dahms, "The Evolution of Settlement Systems, A Canadian Example, 1851–1970," *Journal of Urban History* 7 (1981); Avery Guest, "Ecological Succession in the Puget Sound Region," *Journal of Urban History* 3 (1977); and Edward K. Muller, "Selective Urban Growth in the Middle Ohio Valley, 1800–1860," *Geographical Review* 66 (1976).

3. As Duane Vandenbusche and Duane A. Smith portray it in *A Land Alone: Colorado's Western Slope* (Boulder, Colo., 1981), 55–69, Aspen was "the largest, most significant Western Slope Community."

4. James Edward Wright, *The Politics of Populism* (New Haven, 1974), 167–68.

5. Except for discussions of silver, the economic crisis was absent from the pages of the *Grand Junction News* and the *Daily Sentinel*. Clearly, the desire of the editors to ignore economic problems in order to encourage immigration explains the omissions. Robert R. Dykstra has called attention to the "smoke screen" erected by editor-boosters to hide local problems. See Dykstra, *The Cattle Towns* (New York, 1968), 382–83.

6. Crawford to "Col. McMurtrie," 25 November 1881, (photocopy of original), Crawford Collection.

7. The importance of the railroad to any community's success has been documented by, among others, Dykstra, *Cattle Towns*, and, most recently by John C. Hudson in *Plains Country Towns* (Minneapolis, 1985).

8. Crawford to "Col. McMurtrie," 25 November 1881 (photocopy of original), Crawford Collection.

9. Crawford to David C. Dodge, 30 November 1881 (photocopy of original), Crawford Collection. Hudson has discussed the necessity of currying favor with railroad executives in *Plains Country Towns*, 39–50.

10. Dodge and Weitbrec exchanged memoranda regarding Grand Junction between 12 and 19 December 1881. Photocopies of those memoranda are in the Crawford Collection. Dodge also sought McMurtrie's opinion. He dashed a question—"What do you think about this"—across the top of Crawford's letter to him and forwarded it to McMurtrie. In his memorandum of 17 December, Weitbrec wondered if they had "better submit [the Grand Junction depot decision] to Gen. Palmer first?" Dodge agreed that William Jackson Palmer should be notified of the decision: "I don't think the General cares, but had better inform him as to what is being done."

11. Copy of contract drawn between the Grand Junction Town Company and the Denver and Rio Grande Railway, 17 July 1882, Crawford Collection.

12. *News*, 4 November 1882, p. 2.

13. Haskell, *History . . . of Mesa County*, 64.

14. Haskell, *History . . . of Mesa County*, 4; *Colorado State Business Directory* (Denver, 1885), 253–57 (hereafter cited as *CBD*); *CBD* (1901), 543–50. Apparently, the enumeration for the *CBD* took place in the late autumn or early winter preceding publication; therefore, the 1885 *CBD* more accurately represents the latter part of 1884.

15. The *Grand Junction News* reflected the rapid pace of growth. When editor Edwin Price first published the *Grand Junction News* on 28 October 1882, it contained advertisements from twenty-seven local enterprises, exclusive of saloons, which may not have felt the need to advertise. By the end of the year, the number of firms advertising in the *News* had increased to thirty-seven. (See *News*, 28 October 1882, pp. 1–4; 21 December 1882, pp. 1–4.) At about the same time, the *Colorado State Business Directory* listed fifty-nine Grand Junction establishments. Comparing the advertisers in the business directory with those in the newspaper for about the same period reveals a great deal of overlap; the business directory, however, presents a fuller picture of commercial activity during the first twenty years of Grand Junction's development. The years sampled were 1883, 1885, 1888, 1891, 1894, 1898, and 1901.

16. The relationship between population increase and growth of the commercial community has been studied in several settings. See, for example, Howard A. J. Stafford, "The Functional Bases of Small Towns," *Economic Geography* 39 (1963): 169–70. For studies of the impact of the railroad on community growth, see Lewis E. Atherton, "The Pioneer Merchant in Mid-America," *University of Missouri Studies* 14, no. 2, 1937: 17–20 and 126, esp.; and Hudson, *Plains Country Towns*. See, also, Don Harrison Doyle, *The Social Order of a Frontier Community: Jacksonville, Illinois, 1825–1870* (Urbana, 1978), 88; Merle Curti, *The Making of an American Community: A Case Study of Democracy in a Frontier County* (Stanford, 1959), 225–27; and

William G. Robbins, "Social and Economic Change in Roseburg, Oregon, 1850–1885," *Pacific Northwest Quarterly* 64 (1973): 81–82.

17. Haskell, *History . . . of Mesa County,* 28.
18. Stafford, "Functional Bases of Small Towns," 170, 172–75.
19. *News,* 29 December 1883.
20. Haskell, *History . . . of Mesa County,* 6.
21. Walker D. Wyman, "Grand Junction's First Year, 1882," *Colorado Magazine* 13 (1936): 133; Robert G. Athearn, *Rebel of the Rockies: A History of the Denver and Rio Grande Western Railroad* (New Haven, 1962); 122. In 1898–99, residents of the ward containing Colorado Avenue demanded that the district attorney eliminate "the row." *Daily Sentinel,* 18 October 1898, p. 1; and 10 March 1900, p. 3.
22. The 25-percent random samples exposed the occupational configuration for the community. In categorizing occupation, I used Curti's classifications. Doyle's modification of Curti's categories furnishes other comparisons. James Howard Ducker's detailed analysis of railroad occupations provided the distinctions between skilled and unskilled transportation workers. Curti, *Making of an American Community,* appendix 2, 459–61; Doyle, *Social Order of a Frontier Community,* table 2, p. 261; and Ducker, *Men of the Steel Rails: Workers on the Atchison, Topeka, and Santa Fe Railroad, 1869–1900* (Lincoln, 1983), appendix, 173–74.
23. The 1885 random sample drew no professionals.
24. In both Grass Valley and Nevada City, opportunities for unskilled labor improved over time as they did in Roseburg, Oregon. Ralph Mann, *After the Gold Rush: Society in Grass Valley and Nevada City, California, 1849–1870* (Stanford, 1982), 82; and Robbins, "Social and Economic Change," 82.
25. The same was true in Nevada City. Mann, *After the Gold Rush,* 82.
26. In comparing the economic development of Grass Valley and Nevada City, Mann found that, at first, Nevada City's commercial focus meant more jobs for artisans; later, Grass Valley's quartz mining demanded skilled workers. Mann, *After the Gold Rush,* 138–42.
27. This is in contrast to Doyle's findings for the Illinois frontier, where the proportion of skilled workers declined as the town matured. Unlike Grand Junction, Jacksonville missed in its attempt to obtain the machine shops of the St. Louis, Jacksonville, and Chicago Railroad. Jacksonville clearly shows what happened to towns that failed to attract and/or hold technological and transportation advantages. Doyle, *Social Order of a Frontier Community,* 247–48. Robert Dykstra's study of Kansas cattle towns points to this as well. Much of Wichita's success rested on "its highly advantageous position . . . as a railroad terminus." Dykstra, *Cattle Towns,* 360.
28. In all, there were twenty-seven different railroad occupations listed

in the 1900 census, compared to six in the 1885 enumeration. Only seventeen railroad occupations were drawn in the random sample, however.

29. Based on the random samples, 47 percent of the adult population was single in 1885, compared to 31.8 percent in 1900 (see Table 1).

30. These figures are lower than the national statistics, and much lower than in the mining towns of Grass Valley and Nevada City, as Mann has shown in *After the Gold Rush,* 107–8, 164–65.

31. The notion that everyone wanted to own property is the underlying assumption of all studies of social mobility and economic opportunity. Michael B. Katz states this assumption most concisely: "To discuss the ownership of property, therefore, is to explore the linchpin in the structure of inequality in a nineteenth-century city." Katz, *The People of Hamilton, Canada West: Family and Class in a Mid-Nineteenth-Century City,* (Cambridge, Mass., 1975), 80. See also, Curti, *Making of an American Community,* 55–83, esp.; Doyle, *Social Order of a Frontier Community,* 107–8; William G. Robbins, "Opportunity and Persistence in the Pacific Northwest: A Quantitative Study of Early Roseburg, Oregon," *Pacific Historical Review,* 39 (1970); Howard P. Chudacoff, *Mobile Americans: Residential and Social Mobility in Omaha, 1880–1920* (New York, 1972), 36–59, esp.; Stephan Thernstrom, *Poverty and Progress: Social Mobility in a Nineteenth-Century City* (Cambridge, Mass., 1964), 117–20, esp.; and Thernstrom, *The Other Bostonians: Poverty and Progress in the American Metropolis, 1880–1970* (Cambridge, Mass., 1973), 256–61.

32. Almost identical figures turned up in midcentury Jacksonville, Illinois. In 1850, 10 percent of the population possessed 48 percent of the wealth; a decade later, that same number commanded 50 percent of the wealth. Boom towns seem to intensify wealth concentration. For example, at the height of the Kansas cattle boom, when economic growth in rail towns soared, Abilene's business and professional men—26 percent of the population—claimed more than 80 percent of the wealth. Curti, *Making of an American Community,* 78; George Blackburn and Sherman L. Ricards, Jr., "A Demographic History of the West: Manistee, County, Michigan, 1860," *Journal of American History* 57 (1970–1971):613; Doyle, *Social Order of a Frontier Community,* 263; Dykstra, *Cattle Towns,* 190.

33. Inexpensive property also occurred in late nineteenth-century Seattle, another recently settled community. In one Seattle suburb, lots were priced at thirty-five dollars, and to facilitate purchasers, land developers offered a payment schedule of five dollars down and fifty cents a week. Janice L. Reiff, "Urbanization and the Social Structure: Seattle, Washington, 1852–1910" Ph.D. diss., University of Washington, 1981), 212.

34. This phenomenon of absentee ownership may have been common on the frontier. Doyle found that one-third of the persons listed in the

Morgan County tax records could not be located in the Jacksonville census returns. Doyle, *Social Order of a Frontier Community*, 106.

35. Mann has argued that there was a link between marriage and owning property. Half of the married miners and one-fifth of the married laborers in Grass Valley held property in 1860. Mann, *After the Gold Rush*, 98, and table 17 (p. 240).

36. Operating on the assumption that 1885 and 1900 may be sample years in Grand Junction's first twenty years, I have utilized Chi-square for descriptive purposes. Even so, I recognize that I am using this as a descriptive rather than inferential tool. See Hubert M. Blalock, Jr., *Social Statistics*, 2d ed., (New York, 1972), 238–39.

37. Ducker examined railroaders' decisions about the purchase of property, in *Men of the Steel Rails*, 58–59, 72–74.

Chapter 3

1. *News*, 24 November 1894, p. 1.

2. Because of its late start, Grand Junction benefited from state legislation that not only set required population limits and outlined conditions for incorporation, but also defined requirements for voting and officeholding and the powers and responsibilities of municipal councils. *General Statutes of the State of Colorado, 1883*, chap. CIX (Denver, 1883).

3. See Crawford's recollection of the founding of the townsite in the *News*, 13 July 1889, p. 2. The Grand Junction Town Company, he declared, "caused said town as surveyed and platted [by the town company] to be incorporated under the laws of the State of Colorado, and paid all costs and expenses to such proceedings." Earlier, Crawford had proposed that the new county be named "after Colorado's most enterprising man, a man without whom many of the rich mining regions of this State would have lain undeveloped and probably unknown; he tunnelled our mountains, climbed their summits, and brought prosperity to almost every town along the line of his road, we mean Gen. Palmer, president of the Denver and Rio Grande Railway. Palmer County, a monument he certainly deserves." *News*, 30 December 1882, p. 2.

4. Frederick Jackson Turner believed that the frontier promoted a democratic arena because it provided for increased participation. See Turner, "The Significance of the Frontier in American History," *Annual Report of the American Historical Association for the Year 1893*, 222–23, esp. That assertion has fostered much debate over the last several decades. Recently, the discussion has focused on whether participation is more likely to occur in consensual or conflictual settings. Stanley Elkins and Eric McKitrick, "A

Meaning for Turner's Frontier, Part I: Democracy in the Old Northwest; Part II: The Southwest Frontier and New England," *Political Science Quarterly* 69 (1954), is the best example of the consensus argument; but it has also been put forth by Daniel Boorstin, *The Americans: The National Experience* (Chicago, 1965). Allan G. Bogue has suggested a less romantic but more useful model in "Social Theory and the Pioneer," *Agricultural History* 34 (1960). Others who have examined conflict and consensus in new communities include Robert R. Dykstra, *The Cattle Towns*, (New York, 1968) 371–78, esp.; Merle Curti, *The Making of an American Community: A Case Study of Democracy in a Frontier County* (Stanford, 1959), 300–301, 335–38; and Don Harrison Doyle, *The Social Order of a Frontier Community: Jacksonville, Illinois, 1825–1870* (Urbana, 1978), 11.

5. Ordinances of the Town of Grand Junction, Colorado, 1882, pp. 1–104 (hereafter cited as Grand Junction Ordinance).

6. The same was true for the state. James Edward Wright, in *The Politics of Populism* (New Haven, 1974), 109, has argued that "the [Prohibition] party served little more than an educational function in Colorado."

7. First documented by John Wesley Powell, the role of water as central to the settlement and development of the West has been discussed for more than a century. The most recent scholarly examination may be found in Donald Worster, *Rivers of Empire: Water, Aridity, and the Growth of the American West* (New York, 1985). Other insightful works include Norris C. Hundley, *Water and the West: The Colorado River Compact and Politics in the American West* (Berkeley, Calif., 1975); and Philip Fradkin, *A River No More: The Colorado River and the West* (New York, 1971).

8. Colorado's water problems would be a major cause of the state's agrarian unrest, and would play a part in the development of Populism. Wright, *Politics of Populism*, 32–40; the quotation is from p. 35.

9. Concern for water was not limited to the arid West. Ernest S. Griffith has pointed out that "second only to its relationship to fire protection, and eventually on par with it as knowledge increased, the need for a supply of pure water for health was a motivation for municipal waterworks." Griffith, *A History of American Government: The Conspicuous Failure, 1870–1900* (New York, 1973), 167. Griffith also discussed the controversy between public and private ownership; see 180–83. *News*, 24 September 1887, p. 2.

10. The controversy that characterizes Grand Junction throughout this period conforms to the model described by James S. Coleman, in *Community Conflict* (New York, 1957). Although his model sets up an administrative unit as the focus of conflict, the water company rather than the town council filled that role in Grand Junction. Coleman demonstrates that controversy has an "autonomous nature"—that is, controversies share a series of sequential events (p. 13). Moreover, he suggests that organizations, by being aware of the pattern of controversy, can have greater control over such

events. However, Coleman points out that few decision makers utilize data from other controversies. For an example of a contemporary community trying to resolve its water problems, see Aaron Widavsky, *Leadership in a Small Town* (Totowa, N.J., 1964), 52–71. For another example of citizen participation in community decision making, see Robert Dahl, *Who Governs* (New Haven, 1961), 192–99.

11. *News*, 24 April 1886, p. 2.

12. Minutes of Meetings of Board of Trustees, Grand Junction, 8 April 1886.

13. Minutes, 3 May 1886.

14. *News*, 2 June 1886, p. 2.

15. Robert G. Athearn, *Rebel of the Rockies: A History of the Denver and Rio Grande Western Railroad* (New Haven, 1962), 152–53.

16. *News*, 30 October 1886, p. 2.

17. Ibid.

18. Minutes, 11 and 16 August, 8 and 21 September, and 3 October 1887. See also *News*, 27 July 1887, p. 2; 24 September 1887, p. 2; 1 October 1887, p. 2; and 22 October 1887, p. 2.

19. *News*, 18 April 1888, p. 2.

20. Ibid.

21. Minutes, 8 June 1888. By relocating the station, the entire water system would be within the town limits; furthermore, at least a mile of pipeline would be saved. In exchange for these modifications, N. J. Krusen "expressed a willingness to make some concessions . . . on the price of the annual [hydrant] rental." *News*, 9 June 1888, p. 2.

22. *News*, 7 July 1888, p. 2.

23. Ibid.

24. *News*, 7 April 1883, p. 2.

25. For an example of "good press," see the *News*, 29 December 1883, p. 2; for the negative feelings about the town company, see the *News*, 12 November 1887, p. 3, and 19 May 1888, p. 2.

26. *Keith v. Townsite of Grand Junction*, in Department of the Interior, *Decisions of the Department of Interior and General Land Office in Cases Relating to the Public Lands*, vol. 3 (Washington, D.C., 1885), 356–60.

27. *News*, 4 May 1889, p. 2.

28. Minutes, 12 July 1889; *News*, 13 July 1889, p. 2.

29. *News*, 9 June 1888, p. 2; the quotation is from the ordinance, printed in the *News*.

30. *General Statutes, . . . 1883*, chap. CIX, par. 3312, no. 71. The fact that the council entered into a contract forbidden by state law formed later one focus of the town's defense when sued by the water company for nonpay-

ment of hydrant rental. *Grand Junction Water Co. v. City of Grand Junction* (1900), *The Pacific Reporter*, 60, 201–2; esp.

31. *News*, 1 December 1888, p. 2.
32. Minutes, 4 February 1889; *News*, 9 February 1889, p. 2.
33. Minutes, 4 and 18 February 1889; *News*, 9 February 1889, p. 2, and 23 February 1889, p. 2.
34. Minutes, 31 January and 13 February 1889. These complaints would also form a basis of the town's defense in litigation with the Grand Junction Water Company.
35. *News*, 10 August 1889, p. 2; Minutes, 12 September 1889.
36. As far as can be discerned from existing records, the town never paid any hydrant rental, even though it continued to use the hydrants over the next decade. See *Grand Junction Water Co. v. City of Grand Junction*, 199.
37. See Coleman, *Community Conflict*, 11–12.
38. Minutes, 9 May 1893, and 13 June 1893.
39. Minutes, 14 November 1893. The vote was 136 in favor and 4 opposing.
40. Minutes, 12 March 1895, and 11 February 1896.
41. Minutes, 10 May 1894; *Grand Valley Star*, 12 May 1894, p. 1 (hereafter cited as *Star*).
42. *Daily Sentinel*, 9 October 1894; p. 1; see also Minutes, 9 October 1894.
43. Minutes, 13 November 1894; *Daily Sentinel*, 13 November 1894, p. 4; and *Star*, 17 November 1894, p. 1.
44. *Daily Sentinel*, 20 November 1894, p. 4; *Star*, 24 November 1894, p. 2; and *News*, 24 November 1894, p. 1.
45. Grand Junction Ordinance 38.
46. *Star*, 1 December 1894, p. 1, and 8 December 1894, p. 2; *News*, 22 December 1894, p. 1, and 29 December 1894, p. 1; and *Daily Sentinel*, 27 December 1894, p. 1 and p. 2.
47. *Daily Sentinel*, 27 December 1894, p. 1.
48. Mesa County Tax Assessments, MSS 1885 and MSS 1900, and *CBD*.
49. See Table 12.
50. *News*, 25 April 1896, p. 4.
51. Minutes, 12 September 1889.
52. *Grand Junction Water Co. v. City of Grand Junction; Daily Sentinel*, 5 March 1900, p. 3.
53. Minutes, 9 October 1895.
54. Minutes, 14 October 1896.
55. *News*, 27 February 1897, p. 5.
56. *Daily Sentinel*, 10 March 1897, p. 4.
57. *News*, 13 March 1897, p. 5.

58. *Star,* 14 March 1897, p. 3.

59. In 1891, Grand Junction's population of 2,030 entitled it to become a "city of the second class" rather than an "incorporated town." Accordingly, the council increased from four members to eight. *General Statutes, . . . 1883,* chap. CIX, par. 3362.

60. See Table 12.

61. Doubts about the strength of Grand Junction bonds were not limited to the water company. Following an attempt to find buyers in Chicago, aldermen Reuben Starr and Andrew McKinney reported that "the bonds could not be sold until the litigation now pending between the city and Water company had been settled." Their assertion was challenged by aldermen J. W. Weyer and A. T. Wharton, representatives of a group who, because of their long-term commitment to mountain water, were tagged the "Old Mountain Water Gang" by the *Daily Sentinel.* Weyer and Wharton accused Starr and McKinney of conducting personal business at the taxpayers' expense rather than trying to sell the bonds. (*Daily Sentinel,* 29 December 1897, p. 1; *News,* 1 January 1898, p. 3.) These allegations would take on a more serious nature when, in early autumn 1899, both Starr and McKinney were convicted of trying to bribe Wharton to vote in the interest of the water company.

62. *News,* 5 March 1898, p. 8.

63. *Daily Sentinel,* 8 March 1898, p. 1; 9 March 1898, p. 4; and 15 March 1898, p. 4; *News,* 12 March 1898, p. 3.

64. *News,* 2 April 1898, p. 5; *Daily Sentinel,* 4 April 1898, p. 2. See also Tables 11 and 12.

65. Minutes, 29 September 1898.

66. *Daily Sentinel,* 28 March 1899, p. 1. Minutes, 6 September 1899; *Daily Sentinel,* 18 September 1899, p. 1. See also Table 12.

67. *Daily Sentinel,* 18 April 1899, p. 1; 4 May 1899, p. 4; 16 May 1899, p. 4; and 27 June 1899, p. 4.

68. Minutes, 6, 21, and 28 September, and 11 November 1899; *Daily Sentinel,* 18 September 1899, p. 1; 19 September 1899, p. 1; 22 September 1899, p. 1; *Grand Valley Sun,* 22 September 1899, p. 2. Articles about the various testing appeared in the *Daily Sentinel,* 3 March 1900, p. 1, and 18 April 1900, p. 1; and in the *Denver Times,* 4 March 1900.

69. *Daily Sentinel,* 16 October 1899, p. 4, 22 October 1899, p. 4, and 27 October 1899, p. 4. For details of the state supreme court decision, see *People v. Reuben Starr and A. S. McKinney* (1900), 2d Colorado Decision. Starr and McKinney were never retried. District Attorney Samuel G. McMullin argued that the two had been punished by the embarrassment of the first trial. He further stated that the punishment for bribery was so light that prosecution was not warranted. "Case No. 1141, Information for Attempt to Bribe," Mesa County District Court, Colorado State Archives.

70. *News,* 27 October 1899, p. 1; *Daily Sentinel,* 31 October 1899, p. 4.

71. *Daily Sentinel,* 2 December 1899, p. 3.

72. See "Case No. 1141, Information for Attempt to Bribe."

73. Minutes, 17 April 1900; *Daily Sentinel,* 18 April 1900, p. 4.

74. The erection of a municipally owned water system elucidates more than Grand Junction's political maturation or the solution of a community problem. Such an undertaking also illustrates the sweeping reform movement of the later nineteenth century, when urban reformers wrestled with municipal responsibilities and Populists tried to topple "the monopolies." It is no coincidence that the drive for municipal ownership gained momentum through the early 1890s. While traditional literature about Populism tends to discount "Mountain States Populism" as more a phenomenon of silver than reform, historian James Edward Wright has shown that the movement was more broadly based. Moreover, his study suggests than in Colorado, at least, Populism provided "the genesis and support of Progressive measures." In Denver, for example, several advocates of municipal ownership could be identified as former Populists. Wright, The *Politics of Populism,* 257–64; the quotations from p. 264. That connection was more tightly drawn in Grand Junction. There, activism for municipal ownership of utilities led the way to innovative charter reform in 1909. Indeed, the "Grand Junction Plan" formulated the "preferential ballot . . . to restore majority elections and true representative government," and became a model for early twentieth-century voting reform in many communities. See Ernest S. Griffith, *A History of American City Government: The Progressive Years and Their Aftermath, 1900–1920* (New York, 1974), 62; see, also, James W. Bucklin, "The Grand Junction Plan of City Government and its Results" (n.d.):3; and *The Charter of the City of Grand Junction Colorado* (Grand Junction, Colo., 1909), 3. "The preferential system of voting has been established, . . . thus securing a unique and accurate expression of the public will at the polls, with the minimum of cost and effort. Partisan and machine politics and government are inhibited, and a municipal democracy substituted therefor."

75. See n. 10, above.

76. See Table 11 and Table 12. In Morgan County, Illinois, at least three-quarters of the eligible voters participated; percentages were somewhat smaller in Trempealeau County elections, where between 50 percent and 75 percent of those eligible to vote turned out at the polls. Doyle, *Social Order of a Frontier Community,* 172; Curti, *Making of an American Community,* 336–37.

77. Doyle, *Social Order of a Frontier Community,* 225; Curti, *Making of an American Community,* 342–43, 304.

78. Aldermen in Grand Junction's pioneer period were slightly older than the male population in general, but over time the age difference

increased substantially. In 1885, the median age for Grand Junction men was 29.5; in 1900, 25.5.

79. Curti, *Making of an American Community*, 301; Dykstra, *Cattle Towns*, 237.

Chapter 4

1. *News*, 3 January 1891, p. 8.
2. Janice L. Reiff, "Urbanization and the Social Structure: Seattle, Washington, 1852–1910" (Ph.D. diss., University of Washington, 1981), 127–29; William G. Robbins, "Opportunity and Persistence in the Pacific Northwest: A Quantitative Study of Early Roseburg, Oregon," *Pacific Historical Review* 39 (1970):284–85 (derived from table 1); Don Harrison Doyle, *The Social Order of a Frontier Community: Jacksonville, Illinois, 1825–1870* (Urbana, 1978), 96, n. 5, and table 1, p. 265; Merle Curti, *The Making of an American Community: A Case Study of Democracy in a Frontier County* (Stanford, 1959) 70–71; and Ralph Mann, *After the Gold Rush: Society in Grass Valley and Nevada City, California, 1849–1870* (Stanford, 1982), table 46, p. 266. Mann's table 46 also compares rates of population turnover for recently settled communities; see, also, pp. 210–14. See, also, William Silag, "Citizens and Strangers: Geographic Mobility in the Sioux City Region, 1860–1900," *Great Plains Quarterly* 2 (1982), table 2, p. 171. Stephan Thernstrom provides comparisons of nineteenth-century persistence rates both for the frontier and for longer-settled communities in *The Other Bostonians: Poverty and Progress in the American Metropolis, 1880–1970* (Cambridge, Mass., 1973), 220–28, esp. table 9.2, p. 226.
3. Curti, *Making of an American Community*, 68–69; Doyle, *Social Order of a Frontier Community*, 107; Robbins, "Opportunity and Persistence," 283–84, 292–94. For examples of research that shows a relationship between occupation and persistence, see Ralph Mann, "The Decade after the Gold Rush: Social Structure in Grass Valley and Nevada City, California, 1850–1860," *Pacific Historical Review* 41 (1972):494; Robert M. Tank, "Mobility and Occupational Structure on the Late Nineteenth-Century Urban Frontier: The Case of Denver, Colorado," *Pacific Historical Review* 47 (1978): 212; and Doyle, *Social Order of a Frontier Community*, 107–8. Doyle has also pointed out the influence of stage in the life cycle on emigration in his *Social Order of a Frontier Community*, 112. Reiff's findings, in "Urbanization and the Social Structure," 143–45, lend support to the influence of the life cycle on population turnover, but for a later period in Seattle's development. Robert E. Bieder has pointed out the importance of kin in the decision to migrate, in "Kinship as a Factor of Migration," *Journal of Marriage and the Family* 35 (1973):434–37; and Hal S. Barron has also found that kin relationships

impeded emigration; see Barron, *Those Who Stayed Behind: Rural Society in Nineteenth-Century New England* (Cambridge, Mass, 1984), 100–101.

4. Because I want to incorporate women's experience, I have centered my analysis on the family rather than solely on adult males. As used here, the term *family* includes primarily solitary and simple families. It overlaps to a large extent with the household, but does not include boarders and lodgers. Focusing on the family increases the persistence rate, but by only about 2 percent. Table 13 is based solely on the census.

Table 13
Population Persistence, 1885 to 1900

unit of analysis	persistence rate	N
Total population	12.8%	859
Families	15.0	322
Adult males	12.8	406

5. Richard S. Alcorn, "Leadership and Stability in Mid-Nineteenth-Century America: A Case Study," *Journal of American History* 61 (1974):686.

6. Michael B. Katz, Michael J. Doucet, and Mark J. Stern pointed out the importance of distinguishing between persistence rates and length of residence in "Migration and the Social Order in Erie County, New York: 1855," *Journal of Interdisciplinary History* 8 (1977–1978): 682–83, esp.

7. The Mitchells later moved to Denver, but Charles at least considered Grand Junction his home. He was buried there in 1910. *Daily Sentinel*, 8 June 1910, p. 6.

8. Using the sources that provide information about property ownership and associational activity, each family's length of residence was determined. As long as either the husband or wife continued to participate in the community, the family was considered resident. For example, if a husband remained active in an organization from 1885 to 1897 the family was counted as staying twelve years. Property ownership was more problematic because it was possible that someone counted in 1885 had purchased and moved on, yet continued to hold that land (and became one of the absentee owners). If the same property was owned over time, and there was corroborating evidence that this family had participated in other aspects of community building, then paying taxes counted as persisting. If, on the other hand, property ownership was the *only* evidence of participation, the household was not counted as persisting beyond the first year.

9. Katz, Doucet, and Stern, "Migration and the Social Order," 672.

10. Other sources include publications of such organizations as the

Brotherhood of Railway Trainmen and the WCTU, the *Colorado State Business Directory*, obituaries, and interviews conducted by the Colorado Writer's Project.

11. Marital status was also the "best predictor" of who would leave Seattle, as it was in almost any nineteenth-century community. Reiff, "Urbanization and the Social Structure," 139–40, 143–44. See also, for example, Doyle, *Social Order of a Frontier Community*, 112–13; Mann, *After the Gold Rush*, 211; and Michael B. Katz, *The People of Hamilton, Canada West: Family and Class in a Mid-Nineteenth-Century City* (Cambridge, Mass., 1975), 123–25.

12. Doyle, *Social Order of a Frontier Community*, 97.

13. Doyle, *Social Order of a Frontier Community*, 157; 178–93. For an overview of contemporary scholarship focusing on voluntary associations, see Aida K. Tomeh, "Formal Voluntary Organizations: Participation, Correlates, and Interrelationships," *Sociological Inquiry* 43 (1973): 89–122, esp. 89–91. For more detailed information on the role of voluntary associations in community organization of the nineteenth century, see Walter S. Glazer, "Participation and Power: Voluntary Associations and the Functional Organization of Cincinnati in 1840," *Historical Methods Newsletter* 5 (1972):152; Don Harrison Doyle, "The Social Functions of Voluntary Associations in a Nineteenth-Century American Town," *Social Science History* 1 (1977), 333–34; Stuart L. Blumin, *The Urban Threshold: Growth and Change in a Nineteenth-Century American Community* (Chicago, 1976), 150–65; and Barron, *Those Who Stayed Behind*, 124–27. James Howard Ducker has pointed out how membership in a railroad brotherhood provided an "instantly recognizable badge of fellowship"; see Ducker, *Men of the Steel Rails: Workers on the Atchison, Topeka, and Santa Fe Railroad, 1869–1900* (Lincoln, 1983), 127.

14. In Jacksonville, Illinois, both the Methodists and the Presbyterians had organized churches within the first year; in Seattle, Washington, a Methodist church functioned a year after settlement; and in Trempealeau village, three churches existed within the six years of county organization. See Doyle, *Social Order of a Frontier Community*, 21; Reiff, "Urbanization and the Social Structure," 132; Curti, *Making of an American Community*, 127. See also, Julie Roy Jeffrey, *Frontier Women: The Trans-Mississippi West, 1840–1880* (New York, 1979), 79; Sandra L. Myres, *Westering Women and the Frontier Experience, 1800–1915* (Albuquerque, 1982), 205.

15. Appendix 3 lists the organizations and their dates of initiation. Churches are excluded from this discussion of participation for two reasons. First, they did not regularly elect individuals to positions of leadership; second, the activities of church-related groups such as "ladies aid" societies are almost impossible to trace. Church membership, however, provides a focus for the next chapter. Contemporary studies of voluntary associations disagree on the inclusion of churches or church-related organizations. To-

meh provides a concise statement of the issue in "Formal Voluntary Organizations," 93.

16. The Board of Trade experienced an erratic tenure, and residents hoping to build a local library similarly went through numerous false starts. Each was reestablished several times between the early 1880s and 1900. "The Board of Trade . . . has had spasmodic periods of activity for several years," the *News* reported in 1890, "only to be followed by a protracted 'innocuous desuetude' " *(News,* 22 February 1890, p. 5). The truth of this admonishment was evidenced in the Board of Trade's reorganization in January 1889, again in March 1893, once more in January 1896, and still again in December 1897. Various library groups shared the "innocuous desuetude." The first library association disbanded when the school library was opened, although there was concern about building a public library. In 1894, several "interested gentlemen," many of them members of the Western Colorado Academy of Science, resurrected the library association and "sent 300 circulars home with the children asking parents to donate 50 [cents] or a dollar." When not a single parent responded, the association "was at a loss" *(News,* 3 February 1894, p. 8; 17 March 1894). This group continued without success until 1898, when the two women's clubs jointly formed the Women's Library Association of Grand Junction and later established a public library.

17. "The enormous membership of the relatively numerous orders is explained by their beneficiary . . . features . . . but these societies go farther by cultivating a spirit of fraternity and by encouraging centres of intellectual, aesthetic, and social development, which often take the place of a club." Albert C. Stevens, ed., *The Cyclopaedia of Fraternities* (New York, 1907), 114; see, also, Charles W. Ferguson, *Fifty Million Brothers: A Panorama of American Lodges and Clubs* (New York, 1937).

18. Ducker has argued persuasively about the "fraternal function" of railroad unions. He points out that railroad men "derived from membership . . . a whole range of social benefits quite apart from economics and ideology. Brotherhoods were centers for good fellowship offering entertainment, education, moral uplift, assistance for travelling members and insurance against sickness, injury and death." The "story of unionization on the Santa Fe . . . ," Ducker asserts, "reveals the workers' search for community." Ducker, *Men of the Steel Rails,* 126–39, quotations from pp. 126 and 139. In Grand Junction, the International Brotherhood of Locomotive Engineers, No. 488, was organized in 1888; the International Brotherhood of Railway Trainmen in 1891; and the Order of Railway Conductors, No. 325, in 1897.

19. My differentiation among railroad occupations draws on Ducker's analysis in *Men of the Steel Rails,* esp. the appendix, 173–74.

20. Glazer, "Participation and Power," 157; Blumin, *Urban Threshold,* 172–73.

21. The differences were not statistically significant. Glazer designed this typology for his study of Cincinnati in the 1840s. See Glazer, "Participation and Power," 157–58. See also Blumin, *Urban Threshold*, 167–71.

22. When Curti studied the relationship between participation and occupation, for example, he obscured the discussion by combining artisans and laborers. Alcorn more carefully reported occupational categories, and he expanded the discussion by providing ownership statistics for all occupations in Paris, Illinois. Doyle also supplied information about property ownership in Jacksonville, Illinois, but for only one occupational grouping—skilled labor. Moreover, by collapsing certain occupational categories Doyle rendered meaningful comparisons infeasible. Curti, *Making of an American Community*, 420; Alcorn, "Leadership and Stability," 698; Doyle, *Social Order of a Frontier Community*, 261.

23. Frontier studies have not provided definitions for leadership that facilitate comparison. Curti's criteria for leadership included "political participation in officeholding, more than average total property, prominence . . . in social organizations, frequent mention in newspapers, and prominence in . . . occupational group" (Curti, *Making of an American Community*, 417). Alcorn's definition required political officeholding, mention in newspapers, activity in a booster group, and officeholding in a reform group ("Leadership and Stability," 692, n. 16). Doyle limited his analysis of leadership to those men elected to an office in a voluntary association and cited in either the newspaper or city directory (Doyle, "Social Functions of Voluntary Associations," 336).

24. Curti, *Making of an American Community*, 339–41, 444; Alcorn, "Leadership and Stability," 697–98; Doyle, *Social Order of a Frontier Community*, 269.

25. For example, Alcorn demonstrated that artisans in Paris in 1855 made up 40.6 percent of the population at large, but had only 23.3 percent of the leadership roles. For Jacksonville in the 1850s, Doyle found almost the same relationship—skilled workers made up 46 percent of the general population, but held 29 percent of the elected offices. Twenty years later, however, the skilled workers had increased their representation to equal their proportion in the total population. In 1885, artisans in Grand Junction made up 25.2 percent of the population at large, and held 21.9 percent of the leadership roles; in 1900, 20 percent of the population were artisans, and they accounted for 15.7 percent of the leadership positions; in 1885, men in transportation and communication made up 10.2 percent of the population, and 4.7 percent held leadership roles; in 1900, they were 25.2 percent of the population and accounted for 10.9 percent of the leaders.

26. Anyone meeting Curti's criteria as a "minor leader," for example, would be counted as Group 1 or major leader by Alcorn.

27. Nancy Woloch provides a short overview of the women's club movement in the last half of the nineteenth century, in *Women and the American Experience* (New York, 1984), 269–306, esp. 287–93. Karen Blair analyzed women's clubs, their memberships, and goals, in *The Clubwoman As Feminist: True Womanhood Redefined, 1868–1914* (New York, 1980).

28. *News,* 12 March 1892, p. 8. The Queen Isabella Study Club left a literary legacy to Grand Junction. Out of the membership of this women's club, a third group—the Reviewers—was organized in 1904. The Reviewers still meet weekly in Grand Junction to discuss books of current interest. In a deliberate attempt to sidestep traditional criticisms of "ladies clubs," they serve no food, elect no officers, and permit no relatives to attend. Mrs. W. G. Bayliss, "A Short History of the Reviewers Club," prepared for the anniversary luncheon, 14 December 1938, Reviewers' Scrapbook.

29. The Grand Mesa Woman's Club also persists to the present day as the Women's Club of Grand Junction.

30. See n. 16, above. The controversy over which woman's club set up the Grand Junction Public Library is still being argued. Both the Grand Junction Women's Club (organized as the Grand Mesa Woman's Club in 1895, and still functioning today) and the Reviewers (a literary group that evolved from the Twentieth-Century Club) take the credit. Actually, it took a coalition to bring the library into reality, although the initial impetus was the Twentieth-Century Club. In May 1897, the two joined forces, and "fifty or more of the energetic ladies of our city propose to make the library the sole aim and object of their confederation and organization" *(News,* 1 May 1897, p. 1). "For one year and a half its affairs were administered by a joint committee from the two clubs. In October 1898, it was decided to enlarge the scope of the undertaking. An organization [The Women's Library Association of Grand Junction] . . . was formed, entirely independent of the clubs" *(Daily Sentinel,* 1 February 1899, p. 3). Mrs. Almeda Jay corresponded with Andrew Carnegie for money, and the town was awarded five thousand dollars for a building if the council would provide for maintenance. *(Daily Sentinel,* 14 February 1900, p. 1). For the unsuccessful attempts at library organization, see *News,* 28 November 1885, p. 3; and 17 March 1894, p. 5.

31. All of these auxiliaries also enrolled male members who were members of the parent organization.

32. *News,* 21 February 1894, p. 8.

33. Jeffrey, *Frontier Women,* 85, 79.

34. Nettie McCarey was also active in the Congregational Church, which she helped to organize in 1890.

35. Zona Gale, *Friendship Village Love Stories* (New York, 1909), 7.

Chapter 5

1. Zona Gale, *Friendship Village Love Stories* (New York, 1909), 7.
2. Thomas Bender has suggested *social network analysis* as a tool to understand community more clearly by studying the "networks of social relations in which the individual is imbedded." Bender, *Community and Social Change in America* (New Brunswick, N.J., 1978), 121–28; the quotation is from p. 122. Wendy L. Jones has discussed how networks permit settlers, especially newcomers, to obtain information about other community members. Jones, "Couple Network Patterns of Newcomers in an Australian City," *Social Networks* 2 (1980):357–59, esp. An excellent overview of the network approach to explaining social life is found in Paul Craven and Barry Wellman, "The Network City," *Sociological Inquiry* 43 (1973). For a discussion of its usefulness to historical problems, as well as how I utilized it in this study, see Appendix 1.
3. Jack Eblen, "An Analysis of Nineteenth-Century Frontier Populations," *Demography* 2 (1965): 413; John Modell, "Family and Fertility on the Indiana Frontier," *American Quarterly* 23 (1971):615; Ralph Mann, "The Decade after the Gold Rush: Social Structure in Grass Valley and Nevada City, California, 1850–1860," *Pacific Historical Review* 41 (1972):487–89; Don Harrison Doyle, *The Social Order of a Frontier Community: Jacksonville, Illinois, 1825–1870* (Urbana, 1978), 116–17; Janice L. Reiff, "Urbanization and the Social Structure: Seattle, Washington, 1852–1910" (Ph.D. diss., University of Washington, 1981), 136–37.
4. Robert V. Hine, *Community on the American Frontier: Separate But Not Alone* (Norman, 1980), 147–48.
5. See Appendix 1.
6. John Mack Faragher found a variety of extended families making the trip overland to Oregon or California. See Faragher, *Women and Men on the Overland Trail* (New Haven, 1979), 33–34, esp. See also, Reiff, "Urbanization and the Social Structure," 136–38.
7. The percentages total more than 100 percent because some families had a combination of relatives.
8. Several scholars have pointed out that in the last century there was great variation in the ages at which children left home; in particular, John Modell, Frank F. Furstenberg, Jr., and Theodore Hershberg, "Social Change and Transitions to Adulthood in Historical Perspective," *Journal of Family History* 1 (1976):7–32; and Joseph Kett, *Rites of Passage: Adolescence in America, 1790 to the Present* (New York, 1977), 144–72, esp.
9. Endogenous marriages were typical of small communities, and they occurred with greater frequency in isolated settings. Hal S. Barron found that young people in rural New England also chose marriage partners in

their hometowns. See Barron, *Those Who Stayed Behind: Rural Society in Nineteenth-Century New England* (Cambridge, 1984), 100–101.

10. Jodie Rich to "Mame," 18 October 1890, Annabelle McKinney Dorey Collection, Museum of Western Colorado (Grand Junction), Archives (hereafter cited as Dorey Collection).

11. "Lottie" (Charlotte Crawford Huff) to "Mame," 16 December 1890, Dorey Collection.

12. Aida K. Tomeh, "Formal Voluntary Organizations: Participation, Correlates, and Interrelationships," *Sociological Inquiry* 43 (1973):92–94.

13. Doyle, *Social Order of a Frontier Community*, 181.

14. A sociogram is a visual representation of interpersonal relationships. In this study, the sociograms in Figures 3, 4, and 5 show the relationships between and among organizations rather than individuals. For a brief description of sociograms (or digraphs), see H. W. Smith, *Strategies of Social Research*, (Englewood Cliffs, N.J., 2d ed., 1981), 315–16; and Gardner Lindzey and Donn Byrne, "Measurement of Social Change and Interpersonal Attractiveness," in Gardner Lindzey and Elliott Aronson, eds., *The Handbook of Social Psychology*, 2d. ed. (Reading, Mass., 1966), 463–67.

15. One of the churches formed in the early 1890s was the African Methodist Episcopal Church. Grand Junction's black population was very small, but this church obviously provided a meeting place.

16. *News*, 8 April 1893, p. 8.

17. "Lodges like the Masons and the Odd Fellows were," Don Harrison Doyle has pointed out, ". . . part of national organizations that devised uniform procedures for transferral of members, much like churches . . . . These standardized mechanisms . . . integrat[ed] mobile lodge members [and provided] . . . a ticket of readmission to another lodge." Doyle, *Social Order of a Frontier Community*, 186–87. Ducker has made the same assertion concerning railroad brotherhoods. See Ducker, *Men of the Steel Rails: Workers on the Atchison, Topeka, and Santa Fe Railroad, 1869–1900* (Lincoln, 1983), 139.

18. Barron has concluded that "as frontier regions evolved beyond initial conditions of settlement and rapid growth [,] . . . those who lived there became enmeshed in the ties that bind." Barron, *Those Who Stayed Behind*, 111.

Conclusion

1. Mary Austin, *A Woman of Genius* (New York, 1912), 9.

2. Several recent studies have focused on the community's attributes. Robert E. Bieder has suggested that settlers were reluctant to leave Ben-

zonia, Michigan, because of its religious orientation. In his study of three Minnesota towns, John Gjerde reached a similar conclusion: Church membership was a "restraining factor in the decision to move [away]." Emphasizing another community feature are Michael B. Katz, Michael J. Doucet, and Mark J. Stern, who have concluded that the "presence of economic opportunity for ordinary workers . . . gave mid-nineteenth century Buffalo an unusual ability to retain its people." Bieder, "Kinship as a Factor in Migration," *Journal of Marriage and the Family* 35 (1973); Gjerde, "The effect of community on migration: Three Minnesota townships, 1885–1905," *Journal of Historical Geography* 5 (1979):420; Katz, Doucet, and Stern, "Migration and the Social Order in Erie County, New York: 1885," *Journal of Interdisciplinary History* 8 (1977–1978):674. Robert G. Barrows has pointed to the availability of housing in Indianapolis as an explanation for relatively low rates of out-migration. Barrows, "Hurryin' Hoosiers and the American 'Pattern': Geographic Mobility in Indianapolis and Urban North America," *Social Science History* 5 (1981):206–14.

3. Commercial specialization accompanied an increasing dependence on the outside world in Grand Junction as well as in Jacksonville and Trempealeau County towns. Don Harrison Doyle, *The Social Order of a Frontier Community: Jacksonville, Illinois, 1825–1870* (Urbana, 1978), 86–89; and Merle Curti, *The Making of an American Community: A Case Study of Democracy in a Frontier County* (Stanford, 1959), 224–26.

4. In midcentury Jacksonville, Illinois, almost half of the employed (46 percent) were skilled workers. Statistical comparisons are not possible for Trempealeau County towns, although Merle Curti implies that skilled workers had no trouble finding employment. Doyle, *Social Order of a Frontier Community*, 261; Curti, *Making of an American Community*, 232–33; Ralph Mann, *After the Gold Rush: Society in Grass Valley and Nevada City, California 1849–1870* (Stanford, 1982), 81–83.

5. The findings of all the studies that examine politics suggest that local issues generated debate. In Trempealeau County towns, in Kansas cattle towns, and in the Illinois towns of Jacksonville and Paris, the control of liquor most often generated local political activity. Curti, *Making of an American Community*, 336; Robert R. Dykstra, *The Cattle Towns* (New York, 1968), 253–59, 275–80, 283–92; Doyle, *Social Order of a Frontier Community*, 217–26; and Richard S. Alcorn, "Leadership and Stability in Mid-Nineteenth-Century America: A Case Study," *Journal of American History* 61 (1974):693.

6. Doyle estimated a similar rate of participation for midcentury Jacksonville. See Don Harrison Doyle, "The Social Functions of Voluntary Associations in a Nineteenth-Century American Town," *Social Science History* 1 (1977):336. Figures for longer-settled communities may be found in Walter S. Glazer, "Participation and Power: Voluntary Associations and the

Functional Organization of Cincinnati in 1840," *Historical Methods Newsletter* 5 (1972):154–55; and Stuart L. Blumin, *The Urban Threshold: Growth and Change in a Nineteenth-Century American Community* (Chicago, 1976), 167–72.

7. Lewis E. Atherton, *Main Street on the Middle Border* (Bloomington, Ind., 1954), 42, 43, 186, 181; see, also, 214–16 and 70–72.

8. Robert V. Hine has argued that in a small town people have "face-to-face" contact. Hine, *Community on the American Frontier: Separate But Not Alone* (Norman, 1980), 135–37. Janice L. Reiff has concluded that those people who stayed to build Seattle could not help but know one another. Reiff, "Urbanization and the Social Structure: Seattle, Washington, 1852–1910" (Ph.D. diss., University of Washington, 1981), 130.

9. The findings about demographic changes generally correspond to the model of high sex ratios and an older population suggested for the Rocky Mountains and the Far West by Donald Bogue, and corroborated by others. As an area became more stable, the ratio of men to women diminished and the age of the population declined. Donald J. Bogue, *The Population of the United States* (Glencoe, Ill, 1959), 95–97, 113–18; Jack Eblen, "An Analysis of Nineteenth-Century Frontier Populations," *Demography* 2 (1965):413; Dykstra, *Cattle Towns*, 246–48; Mann, *After the Gold Rush*, 224.

10. Dykstra has noted the impact of women in frontier communities—or what he called the "gradual domestication of cattle town society." "The feminine influence," Dykstra suggested, "increased according to the proportion of wives and married men in the local population." Dykstra, *Cattle Towns*, 247–48. See, also, Julie Roy Jeffrey, *Frontier Women: The Trans-Mississippi West, 1840–1880* (New York, 1979), 79–88.

11. Dykstra, *Cattle Towns*, 365–66, 380–81; Doyle, *Social Order of a Frontier Community*, 86–89. Michael H. Frisch noted that in Springfield, Massachusetts, community self-awareness, which had not been present before, resulted from a post–Civil War boom period. Frisch, *Town into City: Springfield, Massachusetts, and the Meaning of Community, 1840–1880* (Cambridge, Mass., 1972), 91. See also, Robert Dahl, *Who Governs* (New Haven, 1961), 192–99.

12. In all of the studies of small-town household structure, there is evidence of boarders residing with family units rather than in hotels or large boardinghouses. In Grand Junction, 13.1 percent of the families had boarders in 1900. In Grass Valley, more than half of the mining families, and about one-third of the other families kept boarders in 1860. Comparative figures for Jacksonville show that by 1880 about half of the families in that community had boarders. Mann, *After the Gold Rush*, 108–9, 243; Doyle, *Social Order of a Frontier Community*, 113–15. For an examination of the boarding phenomenon in late nineteenth- and early twentieth-century America, see Tamara Hareven and John Modell, "Urbanization and the

Malleable Household: An Examination of Boarding and Lodging in American Families," *Journal of Marriage and the Family* 35 (1973). Household structure may also be a measure of change, and Robert E. Bieder has suggested that perhaps frontier towns "passed through an extended family phase, which under frontier conditions was important for social and economic consolidation and stabilization." Bieder, "Kinship as a Factor in Migration," 438. Decrease or increase in family size has also been utilized as a measure of transition by Eblen, in "Analysis of Nineteenth-Century Frontier Populations," 412.

13. For studies that address the presence of kin in the migration process, see Reiff, "Urbanization and the Social Structure," 98, 136–38; Bieder, "Kinship as a Factor in Migration;" Ralph Mann, "The Decade after the Gold Rush: Social Structure in Grass Valley and Nevada City, California, 1850–1860," *Pacific Historical Review* 41:487–89; Doyle, *Social Order of a Frontier Community*, 116–17, 267; John Mack Faragher, *Women and Men on the Overland Trail* (New Haven, 1979), 33–34; and Blaine T. Williams, "The Frontier Family: Demographic Fact and Historical Myth," in Sandra L. Myres and Harold Hollingsworth, eds., *Essays on the American West* (Austin, 1969), 40–65. See, also, John Modell, "Family and Fertility on the Indiana Frontier, 1820," *American Quarterly* 23 (1971):615; and Eblen, "Analysis of Nineteenth-Century Frontier Populations."

14. Bieder has also argued that in Benzonia kin relationships both prompted initial settlement and impeded emigration. Bieder, "Kinship as a Factor in Migration"; see, also, Reiff, "Urbanization and the Social Structure," 143; and Doyle, *Social Order of a Frontier Community*, 117; and table 12, p. 267.

15. Hine, *Community on the American Frontier*, 22, 26; Allan G. Bogue, "Social Theory and the Pioneer," *Agricultural History* 34 (1960):30, 33; Doyle, *Social Order of a Frontier Community*, 10, 119.

16. Richard Lingeman, *Small Town America: A Narrative History, 1620–Present* (New York, 1980), 479; see, also, Hine, *Community on the American Frontier*, 26.

17. Curti, *Making of an American Community*, 421–24; Alcorn, "Leadership and Stability," 700–702; William G. Robbins, "Opportunity and Persistence in the Pacific Northwest: A Quantitative Study of Early Roseburg, Oregon," *Pacific Historical Review* 39 (1970):283–96; Doyle, *Social Order of a Frontier Community*, 107–8.

18. Mann, *After the Gold Rush*, 213; Hine, *Community on the American Frontier*, 25.

BIBLIOGRAPHY

Primary Sources

MANUSCRIPTS

Denver, Colorado. Colorado Historical Society, Stephen H. Hart Library.
    George Addison Crawford Collection.
    Terry Mangan Collection.
Grand Junction, Colorado. Museum of Western Colorado.
    George Addison Crawford Collection.
    Annabelle McKinney Dorey Collection.

NEWSPAPERS

Daily Sentinel (Grand Junction), 1893–1900.
Denver Times, January–March 1900.
Grand Junction Daily Star, 1891.
Grand Junction News, 1882–1890, 1891–1901.
Grand Valley Star (Grand Junction), 1890–1893.
Grand Valley Star Times (Grand Junction), 1893–1896.
Grand Valley Sun (Grand Junction), 1895–1900.

ASSOCIATION RECORDS

Board of Trade. Minutes Book, 1885–1889.
Catholic Church. Register of Baptisms and Marriages, 1885–1898.
Congregational Church. Register of Membership, 1890–1902.
Daughters of Rebekah. Membership Roster, 1895–1900.

Grand Mesa Woman's Club. Membership Roster, 1895–1896, 1901–1902.
International Order of Odd Fellows. Membership Roster, 1884–1901.
Methodist Church. Register of Confirmations, Baptisms, Transfers, Marriages, and Funerals, 1883–1900.
Presbyterian Church. Register of Confirmations, 1888–1900.
Reviewers. Scrapbook, 1893–1901.

GOVERNMENT RECORDS

1. United States

Bureau of the Census.
    Population Schedule of the Census of the State of Colorado, 1885. National Archives Microfilm Publications, 158, roll 6, Mesa County.
    Population Schedule of the Twelfth Census of the United States, 1900. National Archives Microfilm Publications, T623, roll 127, Mesa County, Colorado.
    Tenth Census of the United States: 1880. Population, Volume 1. Washington, D.C., 1883.
    Twelfth Census of the United States: 1900. Population, Volume 2, Part 2, Washington, D.C., 1902.
    Thirteenth Census of the United States: 1910. Population, Volume 1. Washington, D.C., 1913.
    Nineteenth Census of the United States: 1970. Census of Population, Volume 1. Washington, D.C., 1973.
Department of the Interior.
    Decisions of the Department of Interior and General Land office in Cases Relating to the Public Lands, 1885.

2. Colorado

General Statutes of the State of Colorado, 1883. Denver, 1883.
Laws Passed at the Ninth Session of the General Assembly of the State of Colorado, 1893. Denver, 1893.

3. Mesa County

Mesa County Clerk's Office.
    Register of Marriages, 1883–1900.
    Register of Plats, 1883–1900.
Mesa County Treasurer's Office.
    Tax Rolls, 1883.
    Tax Rolls, 1885.
    Tax Rolls, 1888.

Tax Rolls, 1891.
Tax Rolls, 1894.
Tax Rolls, 1897.
Tax Rolls, 1900.

4. Grand Junction

Town of Grand Junction.
 Minutes of Meetings of Board of Trustees, 1886–1901.
 Ordinances of the Town of Grand Junction, Colorado, 1882–1900.
 Register of Licenses Issued 1883 to 1900.

5. Court Cases

"Case No. 1141, Information for Attempt to Bribe." Mesa County District Court, Colorado State Archives, Denver.
"People v. Reuben Starr and A. S. McKinney" (1900). *2d Colorado Decision*, 428.
"Grand Junction Water Co. v. City of Grand Junction." *The Pacific Reporter* 60, 196–202.

6. Congressional Records

"Reports of a Route for the Pacific Railroad." 33d Cong., 1st sess., H. Ex. Doc. 129, pt. 2.
46th Cong., 2d sess., H. Ex. Doc. 1, pt. 5, vol. 1.
47th Cong., 1st sess., H. Ex. Doc. 1, pt. 5, vol. 2.
47th Cong., 2d sess., H. Ex. Doc. 1, pt. 5, vol. 2.

Secondary Sources

Abernethy, Thomas P. *From Frontier to Plantation in Tennessee*. Chapel Hill, 1932.
―――. "Democracy and the Southern Frontier." *Journal of Southern History* 4 (1938):3–13.
Agresti, Barbara F. "Town and Country in a Florida Rural County in the Late 19th Century: Some Population and Household Comparisons." *Rural Sociology* 42 (1977):556–68.
Alcorn, Richard S. "Leadership and Stability in Mid-Nineteenth-Century America: A Case Study." *Journal of American History* 61 (1974):685–702.
Anderson, Michael. *Family Structure in Nineteenth-Century Lancashire*. Cambridge, 1971.
Anderson, Sherwood. *Winesburg, Ohio*. New York, 1919.

Anderson, Wilbert L. *The Country Town: A Study of Rural Evolution.* New York, 1906.

Athearn, Robert G. *Rebel of the Rockies: A History of the Denver and Rio Grande Western Railroad.* New Haven, 1962.

———. *The Coloradans.* Albuquerque, 1976.

Atherton, Lewis E. *Main Street on the Middle Border.* Bloomington, Ind., 1954.

———. "The Pioneer Merchant in Mid-America." *University of Missouri Studies* 14, no. 2 (1937).

Austin, Mary. *A Woman of Genius.* New York, 1912.

Bailey, Barbara Ruth. "The Founding and Development of Small Towns and Their Main Streets in Northeastern Oregon." Ph.D. dissertation, University of Oregon, 1977.

Banck, Geert A. "Network Analysis and Social Theory: Some Remarks." In *Network Analysis: Studies in Human Interaction,* edited by Jeremy Boissievain and J. Clyde Mitchell, 37–43. The Hague, 1973.

Barnes, J. A. *Social Networks.* Reading, Mass., 1972.

Barr, Alwyn. "Occupational and Geographic Mobility in San Antonio 1870–1900." *Social Science Quarterly* 51 (1970):396–408.

Barron, Hal S. *Those Who Stayed Behind: Rural Society in Nineteenth-Century New England.* Cambridge, 1984.

Barrows, Robert G. "Hurryin' Hoosiers and the American 'Pattern': Geographic Mobility in Indianapolis and Urban North America." *Social Science History* 5 (1981):197–222.

Barth, Gunther. *Instant Cities: Urbanization and the Rise of San Francisco and Denver.* New York, 1975.

Bender, Thomas. *Community and Social Change in America.* New Brunswick, N.J., 1978.

Berkner, Lutz. "The Stem Family and the Developmental Cycle of the Peasant Household: An Eighteenth Century Austrian Example." *American Historical Review* 77 (1972):398–418.

Bieder, Robert E. "Kinship as a Factor in Migration." *Journal of Marriage and the Family* 35 (1973):429–39.

Blackburn, George, and Sherman L. Ricards, Jr. "A Demographic History of the West: Manistee County, Michigan, 1860." *Journal of American History* 57 (1970–1971):608–18.

———. "A Demographic History of the West: Nueces County, Texas, 1850." *Prologue, The Journal of the National Archives* 4 (1972):3–20.

Blair, Karen. *The Clubwoman As Feminist: True Womanhood Redefined, 1868–1914.* New York, 1980.

Blalock, Hubert M., Jr. *Social Statistics.* 2d ed., New York, 1972.

Bloomberg, Susan E., et. al. "A Census Probe into Nineteenth-Century Family History: Southern Michigan, 1805–1880." *Journal of Social History* 5 (1971):26–45.

Blumenthal, Albert. *A Sociological Study of a Small Town*. Chicago, 1932.
Blumin, Stuart L. *The Urban Threshold: Growth and Change in a Nineteenth-Century American Community*. Chicago, 1976.
Bogue, Allan G. "Social Theory and the Pioneer." *Agricultural History* 34 (1960):21–34.
Bogue, Donald J. *The Population of the United States*. Glencoe, Ill., 1959.
Boorstin, Daniel. *The Americans: The National Experience*. Chicago, 1965.
Bott, Elizabeth. *Family and Social Network: Roles, Norms, and External Relationships in Ordinary Urban Families*. 2d ed. New York, 1971.
Bowers, William L. "Crawford Township, 1850–1870: A Study of a Pioneer Community." *Iowa Journal of History* 58 (1960), 1–30.
Bridenbaugh, Carl. *Cities in the Wilderness: The First Century of Urban Life in America, 1625–1742*. New York, 1938.
―――. *Cities in Revolt: Urban Life in America, 1743–1776*. New York, 1955.
Brown, Joseph G. *The History of Equal Suffrage in Colorado: 1868–1898*. Denver, 1898.
Bucklin, James W. "Founding of City of Grand Junction." *The Trail* 7 (July 1914):21–22.
―――. "The Grand Junction Plan of City Government and Its Results." Grand Junction, N.d.
Canby, Henry. *The Age of Confidence*. New York, 1934.
Carvalho, S. N. *Incidents of Travel and Adventure in the Far West*. New York, 1860.
Cather, Willa. *The Troll Garden*. New York, 1905.
―――. *Song of the Lark*. New York, 1915.
Catton, Bruce. *Waiting For The Morning Train: An American Boyhood*. New York, 1972.
Charter of the City of Grand Junction, Colorado. Grand Junction, Colo., 1909.
Chudacoff, Howard P. *Mobile Americans: Residential and Social Mobility in Omaha, 1880–1920*. New York, 1972.
Cloher, D. Urlich. "Urban settlement process in lands of 'recent settlement'—an Australian example." *Journal of Historical Geography* 5 (1979):297–314.
Coleman, James S. *Community Conflict*. New York, 1957.
Coleman, Peter. "Restless Grant County: Americans on the Move." In *The Old Northwest: Studies in Regional History, 1787–1910*, edited by Harry N. Scheiber, 279–87. Lincoln, 1969.
Connelley, William E. *A Standard History of Kansas and Kansans*, 2 vols. Chicago, 1918.
Colorado State Business Directory. Denver, 1883, 1885, 1888, 1891, 1894, 1898, 1901.
Craven, Paul, and Barry Wellman. "The Network City." *Sociological Inquiry* 43 (1973):57–88.

Curti, Merle. *The Making of an American Community: A Case Study of Democracy in a Frontier County.* Stanford, 1959.
Dahl, Robert. *Who Governs.* New Haven, 1961.
Dahms, F. A. "The Evolution of Settlement Systems, A Canadian Example, 1851–1970." *Journal of Urban History* 7 (1981):169–204.
Davis, James E. *Frontier America: 1800–1840.* Glendale, Calif. 1977.
Davison, Stanley R., and Rex C. Myers. "Terminus Town: Founding Dillon." *Montana, the Magazine of Western History* 30 (1980):16–29.
Demos, John. *A Little Commonwealth: Family Life in Plymouth Colony.* New York, 1970.
The Domínguez-Escalante Journal, trans. by Edward Angelico Chavez, ed. by Ted J. Warner. Provo, Utah, 1976.
Doreian, Patrick. "On the Evolution of Group and Network Structure." *Social Networks* 2 (1979–1980):235–52.
Doyle, Don Harrison. "The Social Functions of Voluntary Associations in a Nineteenth-Century American Town." *Social Science History* 1 (1977):333–54.
———. "Social Theory and New Communities in Nineteenth-Century America." *Western Historical Quarterly* 8 (1977):151–65.
———. *The Social Order of a Frontier Community: Jacksonville, Illinois, 1825–1870.* Urbana, 1978.
Ducker, James Howard. *Men of the Steel Rails: Workers on the Atchison, Topeka, and Santa Fe Railroad, 1869–1900.* Lincoln, 1983.
Dykstra, Robert R. *The Cattle Towns.* New York, 1968.
Eblen, Jack. "An Analysis of Nineteenth-Century Frontier Populations." *Demography* 2 (1965):399–413.
Elkins, Stanley, and Eric McKitrick. "A Meaning for Turner's Frontier, Part I: Democracy in the Old Northwest; Part II: The Southwest Frontier and New England." *Political Science Quarterly* 69 (1954):321–53, 565–602.
Engerman, Stanley L. "Up or Out: Social and Geographic Mobility in the United States." *Journal of Interdisciplinary History* 5 (1974–1975):469–89.
Faragher, John Mack. *Women and Men on the Overland Trail.* New Haven, 1979.
Faragher, Johnny, and Christine Stansell. "Woman and Their Families on the Overland Trail to California and Oregon, 1842–1867." *Feminist Studies* 2 (1975):150–66.
Ferguson, Charles W. *Fifty Million Brothers: A Panorama of American Lodges and Clubs.* New York, 1937.
Fradkin, Philip. *A River No More: The Colorado River and the West* (New York, 1971).
Frisch, Michael H. *Town into City: Springfield, Massachusetts, and the Meaning of Community, 1840–1880.* Cambridge, Mass., 1972.

Gale, Zona. *Friendship Village Love Stories.* New York, 1909.
Garland, Hamlin. *A Daughter of the Middle Border.* New York, 1922.
———. *A Son of the Middle Border.* New York, 1928.
Garraty, John A. *The New Commonwealth, 1877–1890.* New York, 1968.
Gjerde, Jon. "The effect of community on migration: Three Minnesota townships 1885–1905." *Journal of Historical Geography* 5 (1979):403–22.
Glaab, Charles M. *Kansas City and the Railroads: Community Policy in the Growth of a Regional Metropolis.* Madison, 1962.
Glazer, Walter S. "Participation and Power: Voluntary Associations and the Functional Organization of Cincinnati in 1840." *Historical Methods Newsletter* 5 (1972):151–68.
Goetzmann, William H. *Exploration and Empire: The Explorer and the Scientist in the Winning of the West.* New York, 1966.
Gordon, C. Wayne, and Nicholas Babchuk. "A Typology of Voluntary Associations." *American Sociological Review* 24 (1959):22–29.
Grand Junction Lodge. Benevolent and Protective Order of Elks of the United States of America. *Our First Fifty years: 1900–1950.* Grand Junction, 1950.
Grant, Charles S. *Democracy in the Connecticut Frontier Town of Kent.* New York, 1961.
Greenbaum, Susan D., and Paul E. Greenbaum. "The Ecology of Social Networks in Four Urban Neighborhoods." *Social Networks* 7 (1985):47–76.
Greenwood, Michael J. "An Analysis of the Determinants of Geographical Labor Mobility in the United States." *Review of Economics and Statistics* 51 (1968):189–204.
Greven, Philip J., Jr. *Four Generations: Population, Land, and Family in Colonial Andover, Massachusetts.* Ithaca, 1970.
Griffen, Clyde, and Salley Griffen. *Natives and Newcomers: The Ordering of Opportunity in Mid-Nineteenth Century Poughkeepsie.* Cambridge, Mass., 1978.
Griffith, Ernest S. *A History of American City Government: The Conspicuous Failure, 1870–1900.* New York, 1973.
———. *A History of American City Government: The Progressive Years and Their Aftermath, 1900–1920.* New York, 1974.
Guest, Avery. "Ecological Succession in the Puget Sound Region." *Journal of Urban History* 3 (1977):181–210.
Hamer, D. A. "Towns in Nineteenth-Century New Zealand." *New Zealand Journal of History* 13 (1979):5–20.
Hareven, Tamara, and John Modell. "Urbanization and the Malleable Household: An Examination of Boarding and Lodging in American Families." *Journal of Marriage and the Family* 35 (1973):467–79.

Haskell, Charles. W., ed. *History and Business Directory of Mesa County, Colorado.* Grand Junction, 1886.
Hays, Samuel P. *The Response to Industrialism, 1885–1914.* Chicago, 1957.
Heap, Gwinn Harris. *Central Route to the Pacific.* Glendale, California, 1957.
Henretta, James A. "The Study of Social Mobility: Ideological Assumptions and Conceptual Bias." *Labor History* 18 (1977):165–78.
Hicks, Granville. *Small Town.* New York, 1946.
Hilfer, Anthony Channel. *The Revolt from the Village, 1915–1930.* Chapel Hill, 1969.
Hill, Joseph J. "Antoine Roubidoux, Kingpin in the Colorado River Fur Trade, 1824–1844." *Colorado Magazine* 7 (1930):125–32.
Hillery, George A., Jr. "Definitions of Community: Areas of Agreement." *Rural Sociology* 20 (1955):111–23.
Hine, Robert V. *Community on the American Frontier: Separate But Not Alone.* Norman, 1980.
Historical Statistics of the United States from Colonial Times to 1970. Washington, D.C., 1975.
History of Kansas. Chicago, 1883.
Hudson, John C. "Migration to an American Frontier." *Annals of the Association of American Geographers* 66 (1976):242–65.
———. *Plains Country Towns.* Minneapolis, 1985.
Hundley, Norris C. *Water and the West: The Colorado River Compact and Politics in the American West* (Berkeley, Calif., 1975).
Jackson, William Henry. *Time Exposure.* New York, 1940.
Jakle, John. *The American Small Town: Twentieth-Century Place Images.* Hamden, Conn., 1982.
Jeffrey, Julie Roy. *Frontier Women: The Trans-Mississippi West, 1840–1880.* New York, 1979.
Jewett, Sarah Orne. *The Country of the Pointed Firs.* New York, 1896.
Johansen, Dorothy O. "A Working Hypothesis for the Study of Migration." *Pacific Historical Review* 36 (1967):1–12.
Jones, Wendy L. "Couple Network Patterns of Newcomers in an Australian City." *Social Networks* 2 (1980), 357–70.
Jorgensen, Joseph G. *The Sun Dance Religion: Power for the Powerless.* Chicago, 1972.
Kappler, Charles J., ed. and comp. *Indian Affairs: Laws and Treaties.* 2 vols. Washington, D.C., 1904.
Katz, Michael B. *The People of Hamilton, Canada West: Family and Class in a Mid-Nineteenth-Century City.* Cambridge, Mass., 1975.
Katz, Michael B., Michael J. Doucet, and Mark J. Stern. "Migration and the Social Order in Erie County, New York: 1855." *Journal of Interdisciplinary History* 8 (1977–1978):669–701.
Keillor, Garrison. *Lake Wobegon Days.* New York, 1985.
Kenyou, James. "On the Relation Between Central Functions and Size of

Place." *Annals of the Association of American Geographers* 57 (1967):736–50.

Kett, Joseph. *Rites of Passage: Adolescence in America, 1790 to the Present.* New York, 1977.

Kirk, Gordon W., Jr. *The Promise of American Life: Social Mobility in a Nineteenth-Century Immigrant Community, Holland, Michigan, 1847–1894.* Philadelphia, 1978.

Kirk, Gordon W., Jr., and Carolyn T. Kirk. "Migration, Mobility, and the Transformation of the Occupational Structure in an Immigrant Community: Holland, Michigan, 1850–80." *Journal of Social History* 7 (1974):142–64.

Koerselman, Gary H. "The Church and Community Life in Early Middleburg History." *Annals of Iowa* 40 (1971):631–40.

———. "The Quest for Community in Rural Iowa: Neighborhood Life in Early Middleburg History." *Annals of Iowa* 41 (1972):1006–21.

Knight, Oliver. "Toward an Understanding of the Western Town." *Western Historical Quarterly* 4 (1973):27–42.

Ladd, Everett Carll. *Ideology in America.* Ithaca, 1960.

Larsen, Lawrence H. *The Urban West at the End of the Frontier.* Lawrence, Kans., 1978.

Laskin, Richard. *Voluntary Organizations in a Saskatchewan Town.* Saskatoon, Canada, 1961.

Laslett, Barbara. "Household Structure on an American Frontier: Los Angeles, California, in 1850." *American Journal of Sociology* 81 (1975):109–28.

Lathrop, Barnes F. *Migration into East Texas 1835–1860.* Austin, 1949.

Laumann, Edward. *Bonds of Pluralism.* New York, 1973.

Lee, Everett. "A Theory of Migration." *Demography* 3 (1966):47–57.

Lewis, Sinclair. *The Trail of the Hawk.* New York, 1915.

———. *Main Street.* New York, 1921.

Lindzey, Gardner, and Donn Byrne. "Measurement of Social Change and Interpersonal Attractiveness." In *The Handbook of Social Psychology,* edited by Gardner Lindzey and Elliot Aronson, 445–67. 2d ed. Reading, Mass., 1966.

Lingeman, Richard. *Small Town America: A Narrative History, 1620–Present.* New York, 1980.

Lockridge, Kenneth. *A New England Town: The First Hundred Years.* New York, 1969.

Lomitz, Laurissa. *Networks and Society: Life in a Mexican Shanty Town.* New York, 1976.

Loring, William Wing. "Colonel Loring's Expedition across Colorado in 1858." *Colorado Magazine* 23 (1946):49–76.

Lotchin, Roger. *San Francisco, 1846–1856: From Hamlet to City.* New York, 1974.

Luckingham, Bradford. "The City in the Westward Movement—A Bibliographical Note." *Western Historical Quarterly* 5 (1974):295–306.
MacDonald, John and Leatrice. "Chain Migration, Ethnic Neighborhood, and Social Networks." *Milbank Memorial Fund Quarterly* 42 (1963):82–97.
Malin, James C. "The Turnover of Farm Population in Kansas." *Kansas Historical Quarterly* 4 (1935):339–72.
Mann, Ralph. *After the Gold Rush: Society in Grass Valley and Nevada City, California, 1849–1870.* Stanford, 1982.
———. "The Decade after the Gold Rush: Social Structure in Grass Valley and Nevada City, California, 1850–1860." *Pacific Historical Review* 41 (1972):484–504.
Marcy, R. B. *Thirty Years of Army Life on the Border.* New York, 1866.
Martin, Robert L. *The City Moves West: Economic and Industrial Growth in Central West Texas.* Austin, 1969.
Masters, Edgar Lee. *Spoon River Anthology.* New York, 1915.
May, Dean L. "People on the Mormon Frontier: Kanab's Families of 1874." *Journal of Family History* 1 (1976):169–89.
McCord, Edward. "Structural-Functionalism and the Network Idea: Towards an Integrated Methodology." *Social Networks* 2 (1979–1980):371–83.
Mellinger, Philip J. "Frontier Camp to Small Town: A Study of Community Development." *Annals of Wyoming* 44 (1972):252–69.
Miller, Roberta Balstad. *City and Hinterland: A Case Study of Urban Growth and Regional Development.* Westport, Conn., 1979.
Modell, John. "Family and Fertility on the Indiana Frontier, 1820." *American Quarterly* 23 (1971):615–34.
Modell, John, Frank F. Furstenberg, Jr., and Theodore Hershberg. "Social Change and Transitions to Adulthood in Historical Perspective." *Journal of Family History* 1 (1976):7–32.
Morrill, Richard L. *The Spatial Organization of Society.* Belmont, Calif., 1966.
Mowry, George. *The Urban Nation.* New York, 1965.
Muller, Edward K. "Selective Urban Growth in the Middle Ohio Valley, 1800–1860." *Geographical Review* 66 (1976):178–99.
Myres, Sandra L. *Westering Women and the Frontier Experience, 1800–1915.* Albuquerque, 1982.
Nelson, Howard J. "Town Founding and the American Frontier." *Yearbook of the Association of Pacific Coast Geographers* 36 (1974):7–23.
———. "The Two Pueblos of Los Angeles: Agricultural Village and Embryo Town." *Southern California Quarterly* 59 (1977):1–11.
Noble, Mary. "Social Network: Its Use as a Conceptual Framework in Family Analysis." In *Network Analysis: Studies in Human Interaction*, edited by Jeremy Boissevain and J. Clyde Mitchell, 44–67. The Hague, 1973.
O'Meara, Walter. *We Made it Through the Winter: A Memoir of a Northern Minnesota Boyhood.* Minneapolis, 1974.

Ostrogorsky, Michael. "An Idaho Model of Frontier Settlement." *North American Archaeologist* 3 (1982):79–83.
Paul, Rodman. *Mining Frontiers of the Far West.* New York, 1963.
Pierson, George Wilson. "The Frontier and American Institutions: A Criticism of the Turner Theory." *New England Quarterly* 15 (1942):224–55.
———. "The M-Factor in American History." *American Quarterly* 14 (Summer 1962):275–89.
———. "A Restless Temper . . ." *American Historical Review* 69 (July 1964):969–89.
Pool, Ithiel de Sola, and Manfred Kochen. "Contacts and Influence." *Social Networks* 1 (1978–1979):5–51.
Powell, Sumner Chilton. *Puritan Village: The Formation of A New England Town.* Middleton, Conn., 1963.
Price, Edwin. "Recollections of Grand Junction's First Newspaper Editor." *Colorado Magazine* 30 (1953):225–33.
Progressive Men of Western Colorado. Denver, 1906.
Quandt, Jean B. *From the Small Town to the Great Community: The Social Thought of Progressive Intellectuals.* New Brunswick, N.J., 1970.
Reiff, Janice L. "Urbanization and the Social Structure: Seattle, Washington, 1852–1910." Ph.D. dissertation, University of Washington, 1981.
Reps, John W. *Cities of the American West.* Princeton, 1979.
Ricards, Sherman L., Jr. "A Demographic History of the West: Butte County, California, 1850." *Papers of the Michigan Academy of Science, Arts, and Letters* 46 (1961):469–91.
Robbins, William G. "Opportunity and Persistence in the Pacific Northwest: A Quantitative Study of Early Roseburg, Oregon." *Pacific Historical Review* 39 (1970):279–96.
———. "Social and Economic Change in Roseburg, Oregon, 1850–1885." *Pacific Northwest Quarterly* 64 (1973):80–87.
Rockwell, Wilson. *The Utes: A Forgotten People.* Denver, 1956.
Rodgers, A. "Migration and Industrial Development: The Southern Italian Experience." *Economic Geography* 46 (1970):111–35.
Rossi, Peter. *Why Families Move.* Glencoe, Ill., 1955.
Rutman, Darrett. *Winthrop's Boston: Portrait of a Puritan Town, 1630–1649.* Chapel Hill, 1965.
———. *Husbandmen of Plymouth: Farms and Villages in the Old Colony, 1620–1692.* Boston, 1967.
———. "Community Study." *Historical Methods* 13 (1980):29–41.
Santmyer, Helen Hooven. *". . . And Ladies of the Club.* Columbus, Ohio, 1982.
Scenes in the Rocky Mountains, and in Oregon, California, New Mexico, Texas, and the Grand Prairies; . . . [by Rufus Sage]. Philadelphia, 1846.
Sears, Stephen W. *Hometown, U.S.A.* New York, 1975.
Shaw, R. Paul. "Aspects of Canadian Immigration: 1951–1971." *International Migration* (1973):118–28.

———. *Migration Theory and Fact.* Philadelphia, 1975.
Silag, William. "Citizens and Strangers: Geographic Mobility in the Sioux City Region, 1860–1900." *Great Plains Quarterly* 2 (1982):168–183.
Smith, H. V. *Strategies of Social Research.* 2d ed., Englewood Cliffs, N.J., 1981.
Smith, Page. *As a City upon a Hill: The Town in American History.* Cambridge, Mass., 1966.
Stafford, Howard A. J. "The Functional Bases of Small Towns." *Economic Geography* 39 (1963):165–75.
Stelter, Gilbert. "The City and Westward Expansion: A Western Case Study." *Western Historical Quarterly* 14 (1973):187–202.
———. "The Birth of a Frontier Boom Town: Cheyenne in 1867." *Annals of Wyoming* 39 (1967):5–33.
Stevens, Albert C., ed. *The Cyclopaedia of Fraternities.* New York, 1907.
Sumner, Helen L. *Equal Suffrage.* New York, 1909.
Taeuber, Conrad, and Irene B. Taeuber. *The Changing Population of the United States.* New York, 1958.
Tank, Robert M. "Mobility and Occupational Structure on the Late Nineteenth-Century Urban Frontier: The Case of Denver, Colorado." *Pacific Historical Review* 47 (1978):189–216.
Tarkington, Booth. *The Gentleman From Indiana.* New York, 1899.
Taylor, George Rogers, ed. *The Turner Thesis: Concerning the Role of the Frontier in American History.* New York, 1972.
Thernstrom, Stephan. *Poverty and Progress: Social Mobility in a Nineteenth-Century City.* Cambridge, Mass., 1964.
———. *The Other Bostonians: Poverty and Progress in the American Metropolis, 1880–1970.* Cambridge, Mass., 1973.
Thorne, Mildred. "A Population Study of an Iowa County in 1850." *Iowa Journal of History* 57 (1959):305–30.
Tilly, Charles. "General Introduction." In *An Urban World,* edited by Charles Tilly, 1–35. Boston, 1974.
Tobey, Ronald C. "How Urbane Was the Urbanite?" *Historical Methods Newsletter* 7 (1973–1974):259–75.
Toll, William. "Fraternalism and Community Structure on the Urban Frontier: The Jews of Portland, Oregon—A Case Study." *Pacific Historical Review* 47 (1978):369–403.
Tomeh, Aida K. "Formal Voluntary Organizations: Participation, Correlates, and Interrelationships." *Sociological Inquiry* 43 (1973):89–122.
Toth, Susan Allen. *Blooming: A Small Town Girlhood.* New York, 1978.
Truesdell, Leon E. "The Development of the Urban-Rural Classification in the United States: 1874 to 1947." *Current Population Reports: Population Characteristics.* Washington, D.C., 1949.
Turner, Frederick Jackson. "The Significance of the Frontier in American History." *Annual Report of the American Historical Association for the Year 1893* (1893):199–227.

———. *The Frontier in American History.* New York, 1924.
Twain, Mark. *The Man That Corrupted Hadleyburg.* New York, 1900.
Van Poucke, Willy. "Network Constraints on Social Action: Preliminaries for a Network Theory." *Social Networks* 2 (1979–1980):181–90.
Vandenbusche, Duane, and Duane A. Smith. *A Land Alone: Colorado's Western Slope.* Boulder, Colo., 1981.
Vidich, Arthur J., and Joseph Bensman. *Small Town in Mass Society: Class, Power, and Religion in a Rural Community.* Rev. ed. Princeton, 1968.
Wade, Richard C. *The Urban Frontier: The Rise of Cities, 1790–1830.* Cambridge, Mass., 1959.
Warriner, Charles K. and Jane Emory Prather. "Four Types of Voluntary Association." *Sociological Inquiry* 35 (1965):138–48.
Waters, John T. "Hingham, Massachusetts, 1631–1661; An East Anglican Oligarchy in the New World." *Journal of Social History* 1 (1967–1968):351–70.
West, James. *Plainville, U.S.A.* New York, 1945.
Whebell, Charles, F. J. "Corridors: A Theory of Urban Systems." *Annals of the Association of American Geographers* 59 (1969):1–26.
Wheeler, Kenneth W. *To Wear a City's Crown: The Beginnings of Urban Growth in Texas, 1836–1865.* Cambridge, Mass., 1968.
Wheeler, Thomas. *A Vanishing America: The Life and Times of the Small Town.* New York, 1964.
Widavsky, Aaron. *Leadership in a Small Town.* Totowa, N.J., 1964.
Wiebe, Robert H. *The Search for Order.* New York, 1967.
Wilder, Thornton. *Our Town: A Play in Three Acts.* New York, 1938.
Williams, Blaine T. "The Frontier Family: Demographic Fact and Historical Myth." In *Essays on the American West,* edited by Sandra L. Myres and Harold Hollingsworth, 40–65. Austin, 1969.
Wishart, David J. "Age and Sex Composition of the Population on the Nebraska Frontier, 1860–1880." *Nebraska History* 54 (1973):107–19.
Wolfe, Alvin W. "On Structural Comparisons of Networks." *Canadian Review of Sociology and Anthropology* 7 (1970):226–44.
Woloch, Nancy. *Women and the American Experience.* New York, 1984.
Wolpert, Julian. "Behavioral Aspects of the Decision to Migrate." *Papers, Regional Science Association* 15 (1965):159–69.
Worster, Donald. *Rivers of Empire: Water, Aridity, and the Growth of the American West.* New York, 1985.
Wright, Benjamin F., Jr., "American Democracy and the Frontier." *Yale Review* 20 (December 1930):349–65.
———. "Political Institutions and the Frontier." In *Sources of Culture in the Middle West,* edited by Dixon R. Fox, 15–18. New York, 1934.
Wright, James Edward. *The Politics of Populism.* New Haven, 1974.
Wyman, Walker D. "A Preface to the Settlement of Grand Junction: The Uncompahgre Utes 'Goes West'." *Colorado Magazine* 10 (1933):22–27.

———. "Staking the First Ranch at Grand Junction, Colorado." *Colorado Magazine* 11 (1934):206–12.
———. "Grand Junction's First Year, 1882." *Colorado Magazine* 13 (1936):127–37.
Yasuba, Yasukichi. *Birth Rates of the White Population in the United States, 1800–1860.* Baltimore, 1962.
Zabel, Orville H. "Community Development: Another Look at the Elkhorn Valley." *Nebraska History* 54 (1973):383–98.
Zuckerman, Michael. *Peaceable Kingdoms: New England Towns in the Eighteenth Century.* New York, 1970.

INDEX

absentee ownership, 33, 35, 108
Academy of Science, 88, 103
Ackerman, Alice, 16
Ackerman, Ella Belle, 14, 16,18, 29, 104
Ackerman, Harry, 16
Ackerman, J. H., xix, 14, 16, 18, 29, 87, 96
affiliate network, 76, 100–106
Alcorn, Richard S., 88
Allison, Monroe L., 37, 51, 58, 61, 62–63, 64, 68, 96
Amazon Guards, 83
Animas Valley, 24
Art League, 105
artisans, 29–32, 111–12; in affiliate network, 105; and population turnover, 79; in voluntary associations, 87, 89, 93–94
Aspen, Colorado, 2, 7, 23, 24
associations. *See* voluntary associations
Atherton, Lewis, 110
Atlas of Colorado, 4

Barnhouse, T. E., 28
Beale, Edward F., 2
Benton, Thomas Hart, 2
Berry, W. H., 136 note 12

Binning, Walter S., 55, 56
Blain, Nannie, 38
boarders, 16, 19–20, 32, 36, 113
Board of Trade, 58, 82, 88, 101–2, 103
Boorstin, Daniel, xv
boosterism, 12–13; importance of railroad, 23–27
Boyer, Ollie Fletcher, 19–20, 99
brick, 29
Bridges, J. W., 55
Brotherhood of Locomotive Engineers, 83
Brunot Agreement, 1
Bucklin, Alvin, 66
Bucklin, Harvey, 36, 76, 79, 81, 97, 98
Bucklin, James W., xix, 8, 9, 11, 12, 13, 18, 19, 36, 37, 51, 53–55, 61, 64, 76, 79, 81, 88, 97, 98, 103–4
Bucklin, Maggie Lumsden, 98
Bucklin, Mary, 104
Bucklin Ordinance, 66–67
Bull, Heman, 68
Burris, C. W., 101
business: diversity, 24, 25, 27–32; expansion, 27–28; pioneer, 13–14, 16, 19, 27, 109; specialty and national, 28–29
businessmen, 30; in affiliate network,

businessmen (*Continued*)
105; and population turnover, 79; in voluntary associations, 84, 94

California, 2, 96; Grass Valley, 75, 107, 114
Camera Club, 88, 103, 106
Cameron, J. M., 79
Carnahan, J. S., 69
Carnegie, Andrew, 155 note 30
Caswell, Charles, 68
Caswell, Jessie, 92, 103
Centennial Exposition, Philadelphia, 3, 8
Champion, Maggie, 18
Chapman, Carrie, 92
Chautauqua Circle, 82, 90, 101
Chenowith, Bessie, 98
Chenowith, Mary, 98
Cherokee Strip, Oklahoma, 8
Children's Home Society, 103, 104
Chinese, the, 28
Chipeta, 12
churches, 12, 82, 100, 101, 102, 106, 152 note 15, 157 note 15
Cincinnati, Ohio, 87
Civil War, 8
clans, 98
Clark, David, 106
Clark, Isadora, 106
class, social, 12, 87, 89, 105–6
Clayton, Thomas C., 54, 55, 56
Cochetopa Pass, 3
Colorado, 1–5, 7. *See also the separate towns*
Colorado as an Agricultural State (Pabor), 13
Colorado Court of Appeals, 65
Colorado Farmer, 12
Colorado Fuel and Iron, 65
Colorado National Guard, 78
Colorado Springs, Colorado, 69
Colorado Statutes, 12, 52, 59, 108
Colorado Supreme Court, 69–70
Company F, 78, 82, 101
community self-consciousness, 71, 111, 112–13

conflict, 52–53, 57–71, 145–56 note 10
Continental Divide, 2, 8
Continental Oil, 28
Covey, Nettie, 18
Crawford, Charlotte (Lottie), 99–100
Crawford, Emma, 98
Crawford, George A., 8–9, 11, 23, 25–26, 37, 51, 54–55, 57–58, 60, 96, 108
Crawford, Thomas B., 76, 78, 96, 98, 100
Crawford, Will, 99–100
Currie, George, 60
Curti, Merle, 73, 88

Daily Sentinel, 70
Daughters of Pocahontas, 92
Daughters of Rebekah, 92, 93, 103, 104, 105, 106
Delaplain, M. O., 69
DeLong, H. T., 100
Democrat party, 57
demographic changes, 111. *See also* population
Denver, Colorado, 8, 12, 69
Denver and Rio Grande Railway, 2, 7, 11, 23–27, 29, 54, 56, 87
Denver, South Park, and Pacific (railway), 7
Denver Water Company, 63
Dickenson, W. P., 63
Dickerson, John, 70
Dodge, David C., 25–26
Domínguez, Francisco Atanasio, 2
Doyle, Don Harrison, 88
Durango, Colorado, 24
Dykstra, Robert, 73

economic development, xvi; business, 24, 25, 27–32, 111; dependency, 109 note 3; occupations, 27, 29–32, 34, 75, 77, 79, 84, 87–90, 105, 109, 111; pioneer, 13–14, 16, 19, 27, 109; and property holding, 32–36, 75–77, 84, 88–89, 96, 108; and water franchise costs, 53–62, 71
education. *See* schools

INDEX

Ela, Lucy, 103
Ela, Wendall P., 37, 67, 69, 88, 103, 109
elite, the, 12, 87, 89, 105–6
emigration (out-migration), 75–76, 107, 114. *See also* population turnover
Escalante, Silvestre Vélez de, 2
ethnicity, 13–14, 17, 20

families, 36, 95, 106, 113, 115; associations and, 84, 90; kinship, 75–77, 96–100; networks, 100–106, 113; pioneer, 14, 16, 18–21, 100–102; term, 151 note 4; transition, 19–20, 75–76, 79–80, 103; women, 90, 104–6. *See also* households; clans; women
farming, 2, 24, 28–29
Feltman, Ellen, 19
fire protection, 53, 55, 59, 145 note 9
Fletcher, Alvan, 19, 99
Fletcher, Archer, 19, 99
Fletcher, Ellen, 99
Fletcher, George, 19, 20, 99
Fletcher, Ollie, 19–20, 99
Fletcher, Robert, 19, 99
Florida, Martin, 54
food, 14, 96; farming, 2, 24, 28–29
foreign born. *See* ethnicity
Forry, Nannie, 32, 78
Fort Bridger, Wyoming, 3
Fort Massachusetts, New Mexico, 3
Fort Scott, 8
Fort Scott Town Company, 8
Frémont, John C., 2
frontier community. *See* pioneer settlement
Fruita, Colorado, 14
Fruit Culture of Colorado, The (Pabor), 13

Gale, Zona, xv
George, Henry, 53
Glassford, Thusa, 99
Glazer, Walter S., 84
Glenwood Springs, Colorado, 23, 28
Gothic, Colorado, 2

Grand Army of the Republic (GAR), 82, 87, 101
Grand Junction, Colorado, 7; additions to, 11, 138 note 11; county seat, 12, 23, 51; incorporation, 12, 27, 51, 96, 100; indebtedness, 54, 63–69, 71–72; townsite, 9, 11–12, 41–47, 115
Grand Junction News, 13, 27, 53, 56–58, 66–67, 78
Grand Junction Town Company, 11, 24–28, 40, 51, 53, 57–58, 73, 108
Grand Junction Water Company, 59–61, 63–71
Grand Mesa, 63
Grand Mesa Woman's Club, 79, 92, 103, 104, 106
Grand River, 3, 4–5, 7, 56, 61, 71
Grand Valley, 4–5, 9, 13, 23
Grand Valley Ditch, 18
Grand Valley Guards, 82
Grand Valley Star, 66
Grant, Ulysses, S., 8
Grass Valley, California, 75, 107, 114
Green River, 2
Gunnison, John W., 2–3
Gunnison, Colorado, 2, 7–11, 24
Gunnison Improvement Company, 8–9
Gunnison River, 2–5, 7–8, 54, 71

Hadcock, Thomas H., 59–60, 68
Haggerty, Kate, 97
Haggerty, Morris, 97
Hayden, Ferdinand V., 3–4
health, 53; infirmary, 12; insurance, 83. *See also* public safety
Hilfer, Anthony Channel, xv
Hine, Robert V., 114
hospital. *See* infirmary
households, 16, 19–20, 33, 34–36, 97, 108, 113, 160 note 12. *See also* families
Hunt, Joseph A., 60
Hynes, John, 60, 102

Illinois, 16, 19; Jacksonville, 72, 75, 96, 107

immigration, 99–100. *See also* population turnover
Improved Order of Redmen, 92
incorporation, 12, 27, 51, 96, 100
Independent Order of Odd Fellows, 82, 87, 92, 101, 106
indebtedness, 54, 63–69, 71–72
Indian Agent, 136 note 12
Indians, 1–5, 7–8
infirmary, 12
insurance, 83
interim residents, 81

Jacksonville, Illinois, 72, 75, 96, 107
Jackson, William Henry, 3, 8
Jeffrey, Julie Roy, 92–93
Jorgensen, Joseph G., 1

Kansas Farmer, 8
Kansas, 8, 9, 56
Keith, William, 57–58, 108
Kent, Amanda, 98
Kent, Celia, 98
Kent, Emma, 18, 79, 90, 98
Kent, Esther "Bessie," 18, 76, 79, 81, 98
Kent, James, 98
Kippe, Henry, 70
Knights of Honor, 82, 101
Knights of Pythias, 92
Krusen, N. J., 56–57, 59

Lapham, Mary, 18
Lawrence, W. B., 87
lawyers, 8
Layton, J. A., 101
Layton, Louisa, 101
leadership, xvi, 71–73, 88–89, 93, 100, 114
Leadville, Colorado, 2, 12, 51
Lesher, Americas, 36
Lesher, William, 36
Lewis, Sinclair, xv, 114
library association, 82, 92, 105, 110
licensing and ordinances, 52
life cycle stage, 75, 77, 88–89, 96; and officeholding, 72–73; and property ownership, 34, 36
Lingeman, Richard, xv
lodgers. *See* boarders
Loring, William W., 3
Lumsden, J. J., 29, 59–60, 96, 98
Lumsden, Maggie, 98

Mann, Ralph, 96, 114
Marcy, Randolph B., 3
marriage, 18–19, 34–36, 75, 77, 79, 84, 90, 98–99. *See also* families; women
Marsh, William A., 34, 76, 78, 103
Masons, 76, 82, 87, 88, 101, 103, 106
Masters, Edgar Lee, xv
McCarey, Charles P., 14, 18, 19, 36, 70, 81
McCarey, Nettie, 36, 81, 93
McCune, Addison J., 18–19, 63, 79, 97, 98
McCune, Emma Kent, 98
McCune, Julia, 19, 79, 97, 98
McCune, Stella, 18
McGinley, William, 9, 11
McKinney, Andrew, 68, 69–70, 87, 148 note 61
McKinney, John G., 99–100
McMullin, Samuel G., 70
McMurtrie, John A., 25–26
Meeker, Nathan, 4
merchants. *See* businessmen
Mesa County, 23, 33, 108
Mesa County Democrat, 60
Mesa County Fair Association, 82
Mesa County Horticultural Society, 82
Mesa County Political and Social Science Club, 92, 103
Mesa Verde, Colorado, 3
migration, 14, 16, 96, 113; immigration, 99–100; out-migration/emigration, 74–76, 107, 114. *See also* population turnover
military, the, 3, 9. *See also* militia
militia, 78, 82, 110; Company F, 78, 82, 101
Miller, A. A., 98, 101

mining, 2, 7, 23, 24, 75
Mitchell, Bessie Kent, 18, 76, 79, 81, 98
Mitchell, Charles E., 13–14, 18, 27, 76, 79, 81, 96, 98
Mobley, Emma, 90, 101
Mobley, Richard D., 8–9, 11, 33, 38, 51, 57, 87
morality. *See* reform
Mormons, 1
Mormon War, 3
Mount of the Holy Cross, 3
Mowry, George, xvi
municipal ownership, 53, 55–71, 72
Murray, Bessie, 98
Murray, Gaylord, 97, 98, 99
Murray, Laura Bomgarden, 98, 99
Murray, Thomas, 97, 98

native born. *See* ethnicity
Nevada City, California, 75, 114
newcomers, 81–82, 106
New Jersey, 16
New Mexico, 3; Santa Fe, 2; Taos, 2, 3
newspapers, 8, 12–13, 60, 66, 70, 78
Newton, Avery, 106
Newton, Martha, 106
Nichols, J. Clayton, 9, 11

O'Boyle, John, 64
occupational structure, 27–32
occupations, 27, 29–32, 34, 75, 77, 79, 109, 111; associations and, 84, 87–90, 105
Odd Fellows, 82, 87, 92, 101, 106
Ohio, 18, 76; Cincinnati, 87
Oklahoma, 8
Old Spanish Trail, 2
ordinances and licensing, 52
Oregon, 75
Osage Mission, 8
Ouray, Chief, 11–12
out-migration, 75–76, 107, 114. *See also* population turnover
Owens, Maggie, 19

Pabor, William E., 12–13
Pacific Slope Ditch, 25, 53, 54, 57

Panic of 1893, 24
participation: associations, 84–94, 112; generally, 108–10, 114–15; politics, 52, 54, 56–57, 62, 63, 64, 67–69; women and, 89–94, 104–5, 112. *See also* politics: public offices
Pennsylvania, 19; Philadelphia, 3, 8
persistence measures, 78, 81. *See also* residency
Philadelphia, Pennsylvania, 3, 8
photography, 3, 28; Camera Club, 88, 103, 106
Pinõn Mesa, 29, 62
Pioneer and Historical Society, 75, 82, 101
pioneer settlement, 7–13, 13–18, 27, 107–9, 111–13; demographic characteristics of, 13–15; economic characteristics of, 28–33; families in, 14–15; kinship in, 97–98; politics in, 71–73; voluntary associations in, 81–83, 84, 89–90, 93
planned community pattern, 11
Political and Social Science Club, 92, 103
politics, 59–60, 69–70, 100, 108, 109; election participation, 52, 54, 56, 57, 62, 63, 64, 67–69; maturation of, 53, 59, 64, 71, 73, 112; public offices, 87, 88, 101, 102, 103–4, 106, 109; turnover in, 71–73; women in, 92
population, 27–28, 103; comparisons, 20–21; life-cycles, 34–36, 75, 77, 88–89, 96; newcomers, 81–82, 106; pioneer settlement, 13–15; shift to small town, 15–17, 19; women, 21
population turnover, 75–81, 99–100, 113–14. *See also* migration; residency; persistence measures
Populist party, 57, 67, 149 note 74
post office, 11
powerhouse, 39
Pratt, J. L., 62
Price, Edwin, 13, 14, 16, 18, 19, 29, 53, 56–57, 78–79, 81
Price, Lola, 16, 78–79, 90

INDEX

Price, Lola Eudora, 18
professionals, and population turnover, 79; in voluntary associations, 84, 90, 94
prohibition, 52, 71, 109
Prohibition party, 52, 67, 103
property, 32–36, 75–77, 84, 88–89, 96, 108
property title issue, 57–58
public safety, 53, 59, 78, 82, 101, 108, 110
Pueblo, Colorado, 27

Queen Isabella Study Group, 76, 79, 90, 92, 103
Quinn, W. J., 101

railroads, 2, 7, 13, 18, 20, 24, 29–30, 32, 34, 87, 89, 109. *See also* Denver and Rio Grande Railway
Ramey, J. H., 70
Rathbone Sisters of America, 92, 104
Rea, H. H., 55, 59
Rebekah. *See* Daughters of Rebekah
Red Cliff, Colorado, 23, 26
reform, 52–53, 115, 149 note 74. *See also* prohibition; prostitution
Reps, John, 11
Republican party, 57, 67, 92, 103
residency, 76, 78–81; persistance measure, 78, 81; property ownership, 34–36, 75–77, 84, 88–89, 96, 108
residential patterns, 16, 19–20, 21, 32, 113
Rice, William, A., 103
Rich, Charles B., 99–100
Rich, Jodie, 99–100
Rich, Josephine, 99–100
Rio Grande, 7
Roan Creek Toll Road, 28
Roaring Fork Valley, 24
Roberts, David, 59
Rood, H. E., 11, 12
Roseburg, Oregon, 75
Roubidoux, Antoine, 2
Russell, Milton, 9, 106

Russell, O. D., 9, 106

Salt Lake City, Utah, 3, 27, 83
San Juan (mountains), 1, 7, 24
San Luis Valley, 3, 7
Santa Fe, New Mexico, 2
schools, 12, 38, 96, 100; teachers, 19
Scoville, S. J., 55, 59
Seattle, Washington, 75, 96, 107, 114
settlement: information sources and, 2–5
Shanks, Charles, 109
Short Creek, Oklahoma, 8
Simmons, J. S., 60
Singer Sewing Machine, 28
small towns, xv–xvii, 109–11; demographic characteristics of, 16–18, 20–21; economic characteristics of, 28–33; families in, 18–20; kinship in, 98–100; voluntary associations, 83–84, 90–93
Smith, George, 53, 55, 61
Smith, Page, xvi
social clubs. *See* voluntary associations
social network analysis, 117–19, 156 note 2
social structure: government framework, 51, 67, 72, 100; institutional development, 81; participation, 76; pioneer settlement, 13–16; pioneer/small town contrast, 108–11; small town, 16–21; those who stay, 76–81. *See also* families; women
sociograms, 101–2, 104–5
Spanish missionaries, 2
stage service, 28
Staley, Lorin A., 36, 59
Starr, Reuben, 68, 69–70, 148 note 61
suffrage, women's, 92, 112
Sullivan, W. S., 62

Taos, New Mexico, 2, 3
Tarkington, Booth, xv
taxation, 59, 63, 67, 78
teachers, 19. *See also* schools
Telford, Sarah J., 93
Teller, Henry M., 58

temperance. *See* prohibition
Texas, 16
Time, xv
Tin Cup, Colorado, 2
Toupaine, Felix, 102
transition measures, 16–17, 93, 111–13
transportation, 27–28
Trempealeau County, Wisconsin, 71, 72, 75, 88–89
Twentieth-Century Club, 92, 104, 106

Uintah Basin, 4
Uintah River, 2
Uncompahgre River, 2, 9
unions, 87
U.S. Census, xvi–xvii, 33–34, 78, 96
U.S. Geographical and Geological Survey, 3
U.S. government surveys and reports, 2, 14
University of Colorado, 103
University of Michigan, 8
urbanization, xvi–xvii, 21
Utah, 1, 2; Salt Lake City, 3, 27, 83
Utes, 1–5, 7–9

Vaughn, Kate Haggerty, 97
Vermont, 14
Virginia, 14
voluntary associations, 48–49, 78, 81–94, 110; affiliate network of, 76, 100–106; auxiliaries, 92; comparisons of, 88–89; listing of, 82, 129–31; national, 83; participation in, 84–94; women's, 89–94, 104–5, 112

Wadsworth, A. R., 63, 103
Wadsworth, Emma, 103, 106
Warner, M. Rush, 9, 11, 57
Washington, 75; Seattle, 75, 96, 107, 114

water, 52–71, 112; mountain water, 55, 61–62, 64
wealth, 32–33, 73, 75–76; associations and, 84, 87, 88, 90, 93, 105; office-holding and, 72–73. *See also* property; taxation
Weitbrec, Robert F., 26
Wells Fargo express, 28
Western Colorado Development Company, 62
Western Colorado Stock Grower's Association, 82
Western Slope Congress, 83
Western Slope Science Club, 106
Western Union, 28
Weyer, J. W., 148 note 61
Wharton, A. T., 67–68, 69–70, 148 note 61
Wheeler, S. N., 28
Wheelmen, 83
White, Allison, 8, 11, 12
White River (Indian) Agency, 4
Whitewater Creek, 55
Whitewater Mesa, 55
Whitewater Plan, 55
Wiebe, Robert, xvi
Wisconsin, 71; Trempealeau County, 71, 72, 75, 88–89
Witcher, Isaac, 82
Woman Suffrage League, 92, 103
women, 110; associations and, 89–94, 104–5, 109, 110, 112; in census data, 21, 96–97. *See also* families; social structure
Women of Woodcraft, 92, 104, 105
Women's Christian Temperance Union, 79, 82, 90, 93, 101, 104
Women's Clubs, 83, 92, 103, 104–5
Women's Relief Corps, 104
Woodmen of the World, 87, 92, 106
World's Fair (Chicago), 90
Wright, James Edward, 52
Wyoming, 3